Reyna

JOHN MASEFIELD was born in and was orphaned at an early age ... School, Warwick, was educated aboard the Liverpool school-ship HMS *Conway*. As an apprentice, Masefield sailed round Cape Horn in 1894; as a result of illness, he was classified a Distressed British Sailor upon arrival in Chile. After convalescence in England he secured a new position in New York. Although he crossed the Atlantic, he never reported for duty. He later noted, 'I was going to be a writer, come what might.' After a period of homeless vagrancy, bar and factory work in America, Masefield returned to England in 1897. His first published poem appeared in a periodical in 1899. The friendship of W.B. Yeats provided encouragement, and in 1902 *Salt-Water Ballads* was published. A distinguished literary career followed, with work across a broad range of genres. Masefield was appointed Poet Laureate in 1930, and awarded the Order of Merit in 1935. He died in 1967; his ashes are buried in Poets' Corner, Westminster Abbey.

PHILIP W. ERRINGTON is deputy director within the Department of Printed Books and Manuscripts at Sotheby's, and Honorary Research Fellow in the Department of English, University College London, where he previously read for his BA, MA and PhD. He has published extensively on John Masefield and been editor of *The Journal of The John Masefield Society* since 1997. His bibliography, *John Masefield – The 'Great Auk' of English Literature*, was published by The British Library in 2004 and his *Sea-Fever: Selected Poems of John Masefield* was published by Carcanet in the Fyfield series in 2005. He has edited new editions of *The Midnight Folk* and *The Box of Delights* for Egmont and his collected edition of Masefield's First World War work was published in 2007 as *John Masefield's Great War* by Pen and Sword.

Fyfield*Books* aim to make available some of the great classics of British and European literature in clear, affordable formats, and to restore often neglected writers to their place in literary tradition.

Fyfield*Books* take their name from the Fyfield elm in Matthew Arnold's 'Scholar Gypsy' and 'Thyrsis'. The tree stood not far from the village where the series was originally devised in 1971.

> *Roam on! The light we sought is shining still.*
> *Dost thou ask proof? Our tree yet crowns the hill,*
> *Our Scholar travels yet the loved hill-side*

from 'Thyrsis'

JOHN MASEFIELD

Reynard the Fox

Edited with an introduction by
PHILIP W. ERRINGTON

Fyfield*Books*
CARCANET

I dedicate my share of this book to my wife.

First published in Great Britain in 2008 by
Carcanet Press Limited
Alliance House
Cross Street
Manchester M2 7AQ

A CIP catalogue record for this book is available from the British Library
ISBN 978 1 85754 913 3

The publisher acknowledges financial assistance from
Arts Council England

Typeset by XL Publishing Services, Tiverton
Printed and bound in England by SRP Ltd, Exeter

Contents

Introduction

Reynard the Fox is John Masefield's Great War poem. It celebrates a
pre-war continuity within the English countryside and rural
community. It revels in the excitement of a chase. It empathises with
'one against many, who keeps his end up, and lives, often snugly,
in spite of the world' and also embodies the image of 'something
primitive, wild, beautiful and strange in the Spirit of Man [that] had
been pursued through most of Europe with the threat of death'.[1] It
is also a narrative of a fox-hunt that is full of excitement and pace.

Masefield was born on 1 June 1878 in Ledbury, Herefordshire.
Orphaned at an early age, he was educated aboard the Mersey
school-ship *Conway* as training for service within the merchant
marine. Life at sea proved a disaster, however, and Masefield
deserted ship in New York in 1895 turning, instead, to homeless
vagrancy. He returned to England in 1897 and, although plagued
by ill health, the would-be poet achieved success in 1899 with
publication of his first poem in *The Outlook*. His first volume of
verse, *Salt-Water Ballads*, was published in 1902 and a second
volume, *Ballads*, followed in 1903. These collections included 'Sea-
Fever' and 'Cargoes' respectively. In 1903, Masefield married
Constance de la Cherois Crommelin (1867–1960), a woman eleven
and a half years his senior. The couple were to have one daughter,
Judith (1904–88) and one son, Lewis (1910–42).

In 1911 with publication of *The Everlasting Mercy*, Masefield
arrived on the literary scene with a new and shocking voice. This
long narrative poem concerning the spiritual enlightenment of a
drunken poacher was followed in 1912 with *The Widow in the Bye
Street* and *Dauber* in 1914. After the Great War further long narra-
tives were published comprising *Reynard the Fox* (1919), *Right Royal*
(1920) and *King Cole* (1921). With the death of Robert Bridges, the
position of Poet Laureate fell vacant and in 1930 Masefield was
appointed. Poetic, dramatic and critical works continued to appear,
in addition to a succession of novels (including *The Bird of Dawning*
and the Christmas fantasy for children, *The Box of Delights*). The
1950s saw little published work owing to illness; however, the final
years of Masefield's life saw a resurgence of activity and success.
Masefield died on 12 May 1967 and his ashes were interred in
Poets' Corner, Westminster Abbey. Robert Graves, in his memorial
address, stated that in Masefield 'the fierce flame of poetry had
truly burned'.[2]

At the beginning of 1915 Constance Masefield decided to keep a journal. It reveals the Masefields enjoying country life at Lollingdon, on the edge of the Berkshire Downs in the Thames Valley near Wallingford. There is also a sense, however, of indecision, claustrophobia and anxiety. Constance wrote on 14 January: 'Oh for the war to end. No real peace of mind can come to one, while so much of the world is in pain.' Masefield himself was 'depressed' and the journal notes on 21 January that 'he is uncertain whether he ought to take some more active part. He has declared himself ready if he is wanted...' During this time Constance recorded an incident that occurred on 7 February 1915:

> ... A poor little fox was in our garden today. He was dragging a trap which had broken his leg. They are beautiful creatures. Yet their whole existence seems to rebuke Englishmen. They live only to be tortured.[3]

Within a few weeks Masefield would be in France as an orderly at a hospital for French wounded. Masefield's experiences of war would also include providing medical assistance at Gallipoli, observing the Somme battlefield, and accompanying the American Ambulance Service.[4] The war undoubtedly contributed to *Reynard the Fox*, but the sight of a maimed and tortured animal in Masefield's garden only a few weeks before tending wounded soldiers may have been the inspiration.

The manuscript of the poem reveals that Masefield started writing on 20 December 1918 and completed the narrative four months later on 21 April 1919.[5] On 5 May Masefield's diary recorded that he had posted the first part:

> Now blessings on 1st part of Fox
> May those who thwart it die of pox.[6]

and the second part followed five days later on 10 May with further nonsense:

> Now blessings on the whole two parts
> May those who thwart it burst their hearts
> And may God make me a better poet
> And give me Time and place to show it
> With Joy to revel in my Fable
> And Light to make my poor clay able.

The American publishing agreement was the first to be signed (on 13 May 1919) with the English agreement following on 26 June 1919.[7] Masefield's diary reveals that the 'last American Fox (2nd batch)', presumably comprising the last of the American proofs, was posted on 9 August and this prompted a rather ebullient author to add to his diary:

God save the Fox
And may the pox
Destroy the locks
Of those who hate him.
May no annoys
But golden joys
Crown the girls and boys
Who highly rate him.

American publication occurred on 14 October 1919 with English publication two days later, recorded in Masefield's diary with an exuberant ditty:

The Fox is out, the Fox is out
So let us sing Hooray
And may he run as long as the sun
And never fade away.

One of those who enthusiastically received *Reynard the Fox* was Siegfried Sassoon. It was during the period in which Masefield was writing *Reynard*, that he and Sassoon first became acquainted. Sassoon contacted Masefield during September 1918 and Masefield replied that it would be 'a great pleasure to me to see you' and continued '...you have done some splendid work... ...I would have written to you long ago, but had a natural shyness, lest I should be... one of the old anti-Christs to be bowled out of the way'.[8] (Masefield's comment may have been a reference to Sassoon's parody of *The Everlasting Mercy* which Sassoon published as *The Daffodil Murderer* in 1913.) Sassoon visited Masefield on 9 November 1918 (as recorded in Sassoon's diaries) and he left with a photograph of Masefield in uniform inscribed 'for Siegfried Sassoon from John Masefield Nov 9. 1918'.[9] Masefield's diary for 1919 notes that Sassoon visited again for tea on 13 and 16 February and lunch on 19 and 25 February. Did the future author of *Memoirs of a Fox-Hunting Man* (published in 1928) provide lunch-and tea-time conversation of use to Masefield in the composition of his narrative? Sassoon was certainly responsive upon publication and Masefield wrote less than a week after English publication 'I hear that you have been saying and writing all sorts of generous things about the Fox. Thank you very much indeed. I am very proud of your praise'.[10]

Reynard the Fox is a poem in two parts. The first establishes the rural community with detailed descriptions of around seventy men and women, revealing minute characterisation in great detail. Muriel Spark commented:

> ...the apparently random selection of trivia is in reality very deliberate. Small sensations are evoked, scraps of conversation recorded, to create the general feeling of something about to begin...[11]

Masefield's method has led many to complain of too much detail. J. Middleton Murry noted that:

> Masefield... seems almost to shovel English mud into his pages; he cannot (and rightly cannot) persuade himself that the scent of the mud will be there otherwise.[12]

True, Masefield doesn't use and develop his entire cast and we are apparently subjected to much detail that will remain unused. For Fraser Drew, however, this richness of background shows the breadth of Masefield's canvas and for Spark 'precision' is 'one of the most satisfactory things about the poem' for 'everything is named' and this 'gives plausibility and an edge to verbal texture'.[13] It is worth noting, incidentally, that the community is so well imagined that Masefield returned to it in later works. Charles Cothill became the hero in the narrative poem *Right Royal* and a central figure in the novel *The Hawbucks*, for example.

Buried within Masefield's extensive detail it slowly becomes obvious to the reader that the historical setting is an English community before 1914. Old soldiers are veterans of South Africa and the Afghan border, not of the trenches of the Great War. Masefield's nostalgia has a purpose. To claim that the poem is a response to the Great War is not to suggest that it accommodates the new horrors of modern war. Its historical setting demonstrates Masefield's nostalgia for a lost country childhood (denied to him by the *Conway*, bartending in New York and work in a Yonkers carpet factory), and places a hunted and desperate creature within the community that went to war in 1914. The pursuit of the fox within Masefield's nostalgic setting is a deliberate response to the atrocities of the Great War.

Masefield's nostalgia also leads him to Chaucer. The 'Prologue' to *The Canterbury Tales* is evident as a model for the first part of *Reynard the Fox*. Many of Chaucer's characters are re-interpreted by Masefield – the Wife of Bath becomes the Parson's Wife, for example, but Masefield, although using Chaucerian diction (note the use of Chaucer's adjective 'verray' for Masefield's description of Charles Copse as 'very red rose flower'), resists slavish reincarnations. The fox-hunt has replaced the pilgrimage to Canterbury and Masefield's community is not Chaucer's.

Whilst the first part of the poem sets the stage with Masefield as a spectator, the second part tells of the hunt itself and the writer, in the view of Gilbert Thomas, becomes a poet and humanitarian.[14] Having introduced the human protagonists Masefield largely rejects them and the hunt is mostly viewed from the fox's perspective. In this part *Reynard* combines one of Masefield's major concerns with one of his favourite devices: the underdog and the race.

The poem received an enthusiastic reception from Masefield's contemporary public. The first British edition comprised 3,000 copies and the first reprint was required within a month. In England alone there were at least eight reprints of the standard text, a limited edition, an illustrated limited edition, a standard illustrated edition, an extra-limited deluxe edition and a cheap illustrated edition (with at least two reprints) in the first twenty-seven years of publication. Later, the poem was reprinted as *Reynard the Fox with Selected Sonnets and Lyrics* in 1946 and *Dauber & Reynard the Fox* in 1962. In the United States the work similarly enjoyed numerous reprints and different editions, including illustrated versions. The text was, of course, available in Masefield's *Collected Poems* which in both England and the United States became a publishing phenomenon.

An early review (now identified to be by E.V. Lucas) in the *Times Literary Supplement* stated that 'This is one of the most English poems ever written, an epic of the soil and of those who gallop over it...'[15] Over three decades later L.A.G. Strong called the work 'the finest English narrative poem of the century, and one of the finest in our language' whilst Muriel Spark, in her book-length study of Masefield, called *Reynard the Fox* 'a classic of its kind; a panoramic record of an English rural community... This poem, I believe, attains the point at which intensity of vision and artistic certainty are equally balanced, and it is a great poem'.[16] However, in 1978, the centenary of Masefield's birth, John Betjeman warned that Masefield's poems 'are probably too long for modern tastes' and noted that 'Masefield did not specialise in brevity'.[17] *Reynard the Fox* might well be rejected by those with short attention spans, yet the ambivalence of the author and his conflict of attitudes towards hunting may prove appealing to a modern audience. As recently as July 2007 a correspondent to the *Daily Mail* called the poem 'probably the greatest of all hunting poems and a classic of English narrative verse.'[18]

The poem was a set text for A-level students during the 1950s.[19]

With this in mind the BBC broadcast adaptations in January 1950, June 1952 and July 1952. The poem works especially well in performance. Masefield himself recorded an adaptation released on a single long-playing record in 1960 and Ronald Pickup broadcast a two part reading on BBC radio in May 1984 (unfortunately not preserved in the BBC archives). The actor, writing recently of the poem and his broadcast, noted:

> In so many anthologies for school consumption in the 40s and 50s the famous and vivid chase sequence always had a place and I remember at about age 13 showing off in class and reading it out loud with great exuberance, a relish and excitement that the much neglected Masefield arouses. Many years later I felt the same but more so. Reading the whole poem is quite wonderful and what remains with me is the feeling I had of being an amazing film camera, capturing a whole community in all its detail and colour, relentlessly and inevitably focussing on the event of the hunt. Aside from his sheer breathless and breathtaking technique it is such a multicoloured and multifaceted evocation of a whole era…[20]

The following year the Young Vic produced a studio production in London based on the poem. More recently, in October 2006, as a feat of memory and performance a former bookseller, Richard Field, committed the entire work to memory and gave a thrilling recital in Letchworth. Mr Field particularly noted that Masefield's jog-trot rhythms dissolved in performance and became flexible lines revealing skilful use of ordinary (or nearly ordinary) English speech patterns.

Reynard the Fox has been unavailable for many years in a single-volume publication. For the present edition I have taken the opportunity to examine the original manuscript and also to provide a number of additional texts as appendices. These appendices include Masefield's essay 'Fox-Hunting' of which Muriel Spark writes 'it is so much a part of the poem that the two should, perhaps, always be printed together; the prose is, moreover, so well written that it could not but adorn the book.'[21] Also present is the text of Masefield's own shortened adaptation of the poem, transcribed from the 1960 recording.[22] The additional texts help provide a context for Masefield's own feelings on fox-hunting.

Ultimately, despite his exhilaration with the hunt, the author remains true to his lifelong sympathy for the underdog. L.A.G. Strong gave an eyewitness account of Masefield telling of the poem's conception:

Speaking once at Oxford of *Reynard the Fox*, and how he came to write it, he told how he was walking one day in a wood and saw a fox's earth stopped up. 'I looked at it, and I thought, "My God! What must it feel like to be hunted over miles of country, to struggle to your safe earth, with the hounds just behind you, and find it stopped?"'

The tension in the voice, the sudden explosion on 'My God!', the force and sincerity of the speaker, make up a memory so vivid that it is the first thing that springs to my mind when Masefield's name is recalled. He has written at some length of the experiences which led him to write *Reynard the Fox*, but nothing in his account is as vivid or convincing as this spoken expression of feeling.[23]

Masefield's joy in hunting stopped short of torture and, ultimately, Masefield could not kill his own literary fox. One of Masefield's correspondents, Lieut. Patrick Campbell, apparently wrote to the author in February 1920 to complain that it was inconceivable that the fox in the poem would have survived. Masefield replied:

I'm afraid you're right. I'm afraid he would have died after such a run, but there must be exceptions, and I couldn't have killed him after he'd gone so gamely...[24]

Notes

1 See John Masefield, 'Introduction', *Reynard the Fox*, 'new illustrated edition' [second American edition (first American illustrated edition)], New York: Macmillan, 1920, p. xvi and 'Introduction', *Dauber & Reynard the Fox*, London: William Heinemann, 1962, p. 78. Masefield first identified his fox with war in 1946 (see *Reynard the Fox with Selected Sonnets and Lyrics*). The idea is described more fully in Masefield's 'Introduction' to *Dauber & Reynard the Fox*.

2 Robert Graves, 'John Masefield', *Westminster Abbey Occasional Paper No. 18* (London: Westminster Abbey, 1967), pp. 17–20.

3 Masefield's biographer, Constance Babington Smith, transcribed parts of Constance Masefield's diaries. These transcriptions are preserved in The Archives of the John Masefield Society. All quotations are taken from this typescript source.

4 Masefield's Great War experiences are detailed within *John Masefield's Great War: Collected Works* (edited with an introduction by Philip W. Errington) (Barnsley: Pen and Sword Military Classics, 2007).

5 Recorded by Masefield on the title-page of his manuscript notebook (see Bodleian MSS. Eng.Poet e.116–118). In his essay 'Fox-Hunting' Masefield provides different dates.

6 Masefield's sketchy 'Pocket Diary and Note Book for 1919' is preserved within the Harry Ransom Humanities Research Center, University of Texas.

7 See Errington, Philip W. *John Masefield – The 'Great Auk' of English Literature* (London: The British Library, 2004), pp. 187–88).

8 Masefield, John. ALS to Siegfried Sassoon, 5 September 1918 (Cambridge University Library. Add.8889/3, f. 229).

9 See Sotheby's auction catalogue, 18 July 1991, lot 90.

10 Masefield, John. ALS to Siegfried Sassoon, 22 October 1918 (Cambridge University Library. Add.8889/3, f. 237).

11 Spark, Muriel. *John Masefield* (London: Peter Nevill, 1953), p. 158.

12 Murry, J. Middleton. *Aspects of Literature* (London: Collins, 1920), p. 154.

13 See Drew, Fraser. *John Masefield's England – A Study of the National Themes in His Work* (Cranbury, New Jersey: Associated University Presses, 1973) and Spark, Muriel; *John Masefield* (London: Peter Nevill, 1953), p. 161.

14 Thomas, Gilbert. *John Masefield* (London: Thornton Butterworth, [1931]), p. 194.

15 *Times Literary Supplement*, 23 October 1919, p. 586. The author is identified by the TLS Centenary Archive.

16 See Strong, L.A.G. *John Masefield* (London: Longmans, Green and Co., 1952), p. 23 and Spark, Muriel; *John Masefield* (London: Peter Nevill, 1953), p. 17.

17 Betjeman, John. Preface to Masefield, John; *Selected Poems* (London: Heinemann, 1978), p. viii.

18 *Daily Mail*, 26 July 2007, p. 61.

19 *The Guardian* for 23 October 2006 (see G2, p. 15) listed set texts for the University of London Exam board and its successor, Edexcel, in 1953, 1975, 1986 and 2006. Masefield featured only in 1953.

20 Pickup, Ronald. ALS to Philip W. Errington, 6 November 2006.

21 Spark, Muriel. *John Masefield* (London: Peter Nevill, 1953), p. 156.

22 The text of the poem as rendered here does not transcribe any of Masefield's minor changes or flaws in performance. It does, however, reveal some significant reworking of the text in places.

23 Strong, L.A.G. *John Masefield* (London: Longmans, Green and Co., 1952), pp. 9–10.

24 Masefield, John. ALS to [Patrick] Campbell, 20 February 1920 (Archives of The John Masefield Society).

Note on the Text

An editor of *Reynard the Fox* has much potential material at his disposal.

The original autograph manuscript is written in three linen-covered notebooks.[1] These notebooks show the process of creation with extensive deletions, insertions and other corrections. Pages (or sections of pages) are removed or other slips of paper are laid down over other material.

The deletions removed from the notebooks survive in an envelope marked 'The Fox. Rejections'.[2] These comprise a sheaf of single sheets or cuttings and suggest that the poem was originally a first-person narrative with the narrator beginning his tale before the day of the hunt:

> The night came full of scents of things
> The rooks fell still and shut their wings
> The wind died in the elm-tree boughs
> And lamp light came in huntsman's house
> So homelike that it touched my heart.
> Down in the road a jogging cart
> Bumped home, the driver singing plain.
> The wet red sunset promised rain.
> The air was fat with it I felt
> The earth foretell rain as I smelt…

> …So warm so moist the air I felt rain coming
> It was so warm and moist, the smell
> Blent with the noises to foretell
> Soft weather for the coming day
> Wafts from the byre of mulch and hay
> Came warm, I heard the bells begin
> I heard Black Rachel at the inn
> Six hundred yards from where I stood.
> Owls started hunting in the wood.

> And as an owl hallooed I heard
> A hound give answer to the bird
> As though that tremulous wild horn
> Blew in a pack by Dead Man's Thorn
> Heads down, sterns waving, hearts intent…

These deletions have not, however, been used in the editorial process and I have not restored material that the author decided to omit.

There is also a typescript of 67 pages (top copy and carbon) marked 'Reynard the Fox. Typescript'.[3] I suspect this may comprise the first typescript version although a number of leaves were later re-typed since some strikes of occasional letters show sufficient differences in alignment from the other typescripts. There are a small number of authorial corrections.

A second typescript of 67 pages (top copy and carbon) is marked 'Typescript from which it was set in America'.[4] There are a small number of authorial corrections.

A third typescript of 67 pages (mostly top copy) is marked 'Typescript from which it was set in England' with an ink stamp from William Heinemann noting that it was received on 6 June 1919.[5] This is marked with a series of names, presumably those of the compositors. There are a small number of authorial corrections.

Another source of material comprises a set of undated bound galley proofs marked 'American Proofs' in which two pages appear side by side on each leaf.[6] These include no significant markings. It is assumed that any proofs annotated by the author were returned to the printers.

The typescripts reveal errors on the part of the typist that, unnoticed, appear in the published text. Yet there are also examples of substantive corrections that appear within the typescripts.

It must be assumed, therefore, that Masefield corrected each typescript (usually, but not always, with the same changes) and changed American and English proofs separately. Variants therefore abound between different versions. My editorial intention has been to produce a text based on the manuscript but informed by the three typescript versions, American proof and first American and English editions. I have chosen to ignore all subsequent publications of the poem during Masefield's lifetime.

In Masefield's manuscript, division into stanzas is frequently shown by a horizontal line (with two vertical dashes at the centre). These divisions were rendered in the typescript as three asterisks and tend to be preserved in the English first edition by a series of four asterisks. For this edition I have chosen to remove all marking of stanza divisions except the standard convention of a blank line, although instructions for text to start on a new page have been followed. To conform with modern practice, single quote marks have replaced double. I have retained a distinct feature of Masefield's diction. One rather opinionated critic has complained against Masefield's 'maddening quaintness of spelling, such as his late 1920s fad for verbs like "laught", "reacht" and "watcht" '.[7] These are in the manuscript and all subsequent substantive editions. They add a distinctive clipped feel to the text and I have retained the author's chosen poetic diction.

I have, in general, followed the manuscript adding corrections or changes in firstly, the American and then, the English edition. A number of substantive differences suggest this ordering. The 'cold eye' of Old Bennett in the first part of the poem, for example 'reached the women through' in both editions (and all typescripts). The manuscript clearly reads 'searched the women through'. Old Baldy Hill's advice to Sir Peter Bynd is concluded with the suggestion 'Heath Wood, Sir Peter's best to draw'. The accurate reading, from the manuscript, is 'Heath Wood, Sir Peter, 's best to draw'. The error originates from the typescripts. Earlier in this part of the poem Jill and Joan are 'as bright as fresh sweet-peas' in the manuscript and American edition. The English edition includes a typographical error reading 'bright as as fresh sweet-peas'. White Rabbit is 'stanch' in the English edition and has continued to be so for every English edition until now. In America and the manuscript he is the more familiar variant 'staunch'.

The American first edition follows the manuscript more closely than the English first. The American edition was published by Macmillan on 14 October 1919 with English publication by Heinemann two days later. The English edition is more heavily punctuated and I have tended to remove much additional punctuation. Although the typescript for Heinemann includes many – but not all – punctuation marks, these are not, necessarily, authorial. Masefield may have had greater opportunity to tweak the English setting. Did he, for example, correct proofs for Heinemann? (The dedication to the Galsworthys is, for example lacking in all textual sources except the first English edition.)

This current edition therefore reverts, largely, to the manuscript. The manuscript and American editions are lightly punctuated and this helps a freer, less staccato rhythm throughout.

Notes
1 Bodleian MSS. Eng.Poet e.116–118.
2 Bodleian. Dep.c.307. I am extremely grateful to Mr W.H. Masefield for permission to consult this material.
3 Bodleian. Dep.d.255.
4 Bodleian. Dep.d.254.
5 Bodleian. Dep.c.307.
6 Bodleian. Dep.c.337.
7 See *TLS*, 3 June 2005, p. 7.

Reynard the Fox

To Ada and John Galsworthy

Part I

The meet was at 'The Cock and Pye
By Charles and Martha Enderby,'
The grey, three-hundred-year-old inn
Long since the haunt of Benjamin,
The highwayman who rode the bay.
The tavern fronts the coaching way,
The mail changed horses there of old.
It has a strip of grassy mould
In front of it, a broad green strip.
A trough, where horses' muzzles dip,
Stands opposite the tavern front,
And there that morning came the hunt,
To fill that quiet width of road
As full of men as Framilode
Is full of sea when tide is in.

The stables were alive with din
From dawn until the time of meeting.
A pad-groom gave a cloth a beating,
Knocking the dust out with a stake.
Two men cleaned stalls with fork and rake,
And one went whistling to the pump,
The handle whined, ker-lump, ker-lump,
The water splashed into the pail,
And, as he went, it left a trail,
Lipped over on the yard's bricked paving.
Two grooms (sent on before) were shaving
There in the yard, at glasses propped
On jutting bricks; they scraped and stropped,
And felt their chins and leaned and peered,
A woodland day was what they feared
(As second horsemen), shaving there.
Then, in the stalls where hunters were,
Straw rustled as the horses shifted,
The hayseeds ticked and haystraws drifted
From racks as horses tugged their feed.
Slow gulping sounds of steady greed

Came from each stall, and sometimes stampings,
Whinnies (at well-known steps) and rampings
To see the horse in the next stall.

Outside, the spangled cock did call
To scattering grain that Martha flung.
And many a time a mop was wrung
By Susan ere the floor was clean.
The harness-room, that busy scene,
Clinked and chinked from ostlers brightening
Rings and bits with dips of whitening,
Rubbing fox-flecks out of stirrups,
Dumbing buckles of their chirrups
By the touch of oily feathers.
Some, with stag's bones rubbed at leathers,
Brushed at saddle-flaps or hove
Saddle-linings to the stove.
Blue smoke from strong tobacco drifted
Out of the yard, the passers snifft it,
Mixed with the strong ammonia flavour
Of horses' stables and the savour
Of saddle-paste and polish spirit
Which put the gleam on flap and tirrit.
The grooms in shirts with rolled-up sleeves,
Belted by girths of coloured weaves,
Groomed the clipped hunters in their stalls.
One said, 'My dad cured saddle galls,
He called it Doctor Barton's cure –
Hog's lard and borax, laid on pure.'
And others said, 'Ge' back, my son,'
'Stand over, girl; now, girl, ha' done.'
'Now, boy, no snapping; gently. Crikes
He gives a rare pinch when he likes.'
'Drawn blood? I thought he looked a biter.'
'I give 'em all sweet spit of nitre
For that, myself: that sometimes cures.'
'Now, Beauty, mind them feet of yours.'
They groomed, and sissed with hissing notes
To keep the dust out of their throats.

There came again and yet again
The feed-box lid, the swish of grain,
Or Joe's boots stamping in the loft,
The hay-fork's stab and then the soft

4

Hay's scratching slither down the shoot.
Then with a thud some horse's foot
Stamped, and the gulping munch again
Resumed its lippings at the grain.

The road outside the inn was quiet
Save for the poor, mad, restless pyat
Hopping his hanging wicker-cage.
No calmative of sleep or sage
Will cure the fever to be free.
He shook the wicker ceaselessly
Now up, now down, but never out
On wind-waves, being blown about,
Looking for dead things good to eat.
His cage was strewn with scattered wheat.

At ten o'clock, the doctor's lad
Brought up his master's hunting pad
And put him in a stall, and leaned
Against the stall, and sissed, and cleaned
The port and cannons of his curb.
He chewed a sprig of smelling herb.
He sometimes stopped, and spat, and chid
The silly things his master did.

At twenty past, old Baldock strode
His ploughman's straddle down the road.
An old man with a gaunt, burnt face.
His eyes rapt back on some far place
Like some starved, half-mad saint in bliss
In God's world through the rags of this.
He leaned upon a stake of ash
Cut from a sapling: many a gash
Was in his old, full-skirted coat.
The twisted muscles in his throat
Moved, as he swallowed, like taut cord.
His oaken face was seamed and gored;
He halted by the inn and stared
On that far bliss, that place prepared
Beyond his eyes, beyond his mind.

Then Thomas Copp, of Cowfoot's Wynd,
Drove up; and stopped to take a glass.
'I hope they'll gallop on my grass,'

He said, 'My little girl does sing
To see the red coats galloping.
It's good for grass, too, to be trodden
Except they poach it, where it's sodden.'

Then Billy Waldrist, from the Lynn,
With Jockey Hill, from Pitts, came in
And had a sip of gin and stout
To help the jockey's sweatings out.
'Rare day for scent,' the jockey said.

A pony like a feather bed
On four short sticks, took place aside.
The little girl who rode astride
Watched everything with eyes that glowed
With glory in the horse she rode.

At half-past ten, some lads on foot
Came to be beaters to a shoot
Of rabbits on the Warren Hill.
Rough sticks they had, and Hob and Jill,
Their ferrets, in a bag, and netting.
They talked of dinner-beer and betting;
And jeered at those who stood around.
They rolled their dogs upon the ground
And teased them: 'Rats;' they cried, 'Go fetch.'
'Go seek, good Roxer; 'z bite, good betch.
What dinner-beer'll they give us, lad?
Sex quarts the lot last year we had.
They'd ought to give us seven this.
Seek, Susan; what a betch it is.'

A pommle cob came trotting up
Round-bellied like a drinking-cup,
Bearing on back a pommle man
Round-bellied like a drinking can,
The clergyman from Condicote.
His face was scarlet from his trot,
His white hair bobbed about his head
As halos do round clergy dead.
He asked Tom Copp, 'How long to wait?'
His loose mouth opened like a gate,
To pass the wagons of his speech,
He had a mighty voice to preach

Though indolent in other matters.
He let his children go in tatters.

His daughter Madge on foot, flush-cheekt,
In broken hat and boots that leakt,
With bits of hay all over her,
Her plain face grinning at the stir
(A broad pale face, snub-nosed, with speckles
Of sandy eyebrows sprinkt with freckles)
Came after him and stood apart
Beside the darling of her heart,
Miss Hattie Dyce from Baydon Dean,
A big young fair one, chiselled clean
Brow, chin and nose, with great blue eyes
All innocence and sweet surprise
And golden hair piled coil on coil
Too beautiful for time to spoil.
They talked in undertones together
Not of the hunting, nor the weather.

Old Steven from Scratch Steven Place
(A white beard and a rosy face)
Came next on his stringhalty grey,
'I've come to see the hounds away,'
He said, 'And ride a field or two.
We old have better things to do
Than breaking all our necks for fun.'
He shone on people like the sun,
And on himself for shining so.

Three men came riding in a row:–
John Pym, a bull-man, quick to strike,
Gross and blunt-headed like a shrike
Yet sweet-voiced as a piping flute;
Tom See, the trainer, from the Toot,
Red, with an angry, puzzled face
And mouth twitched upward out of place
Sucking cheap grapes and spitting seeds;
And Stone, of Bartle's Cattle Feeds,
A man whose bulk of flesh and bone
Made people call him Twenty Stone.
He was the man who stood a pull
At Tencombe with the Jersey bull
And brought the bull back to his stall.

7

Some children ranged the tavern-wall.
Sucking their thumbs and staring hard;
Some grooms brought horses from the yard.
Jane Selbie said to Ellen Tranter,
'A lot on 'em come doggin', ant her?'
'A lot on 'em,' said Ellen, 'Look.
There'm Mr Gaunt of Water's Hook.
They say he...' (whispered). 'Law,' said Jane.
Gaunt flung his heel across the mane,
And slithered from his horse and stamped.
'Boots tight,' he said, 'my feet are cramped.'

A loose-shod horse came clicking clack;
Nick Wolvesey on a hired hack
Came tittup, like a cup and ball.
One saw the sun, moon, stars and all
The great green earth twixt him and saddle;
Then Molly Wolvesey riding straddle
Red as a rose, with eyes like sparks,
Two boys from college out for larks
Hunted bright Molly for a smile
But were not worth their quarry's while.

Two eye-glassed gunners dressed in tweed
Came with a spaniel on a lead
And waited for a fellow-gunner.

The parson's son, the famous runner,
Came dressed to follow hounds on foot.
His knees were red as yew tree root
From being bare, day in day out,
He wore a blazer, and a clout
(His sweater's arms) tied round his neck.
His football shorts had many a speck
And splash of mud from many a fall
Got as he picked the slippery ball
Heeled out behind a breaking scrum.
He grinned at people, but was dumb,
Not like these lousy foreigners.
The otter-hounds and harriers
From Godstow to the Wye all knew him.

And with him came the stock which grew him,
The parson and his sporting wife,
She was a stout one, full of life

With red, quick, kindly, manly face.
She held the knave, queen, king and ace,
In every hand she played with men.
She was no sister to the hen,
But fierce and minded to be queen.
She wore a coat and skirt of green,
A waistcoat cut of hunting red,
Her tie pin was a fox's head.

The parson was a manly one
His jolly eyes were bright with fun.
His jolly mouth was well inclined
To cry aloud his jolly mind
To everyone, in jolly terms.
He did not talk of churchyard worms
But of our privilege as dust
To box a lively bout with lust
Ere going to Heaven to rejoice.
He loved the sound of his own voice.
His talk was like a charge of horse
His build was all compact, for force,
Well-knit, well-made, well-coloured, eager,
He kept no Lent to make him meagre.
He loved his God, himself and man
He never said, 'Life's wretched span;
This wicked world,' in any sermon.
This body that we feed the worm on,
To him, was jovial stuff that thrilled.
He liked to see the foxes killed;
But most he felt himself in clover
To hear, 'Hen left, hare right, cock over,'
At woodside, when the leaves are brown.
Some grey cathedral in a town
Where drowsy bells toll out the time
To shaven closes sweet with lime
And wall-flower roots rive out the mortar
All summer on the Norman dortar
Was certain someday to be his.
Nor would a mitre go amiss
To him, because he governed well.
His voice was like the tenor bell
When services were said and sung.
And he had read in many a tongue,
Arabic, Hebrew, Spanish, Greek.

Two bright young women, nothing meek,
Rode up on bicycles and propped
Their wheels in such wise that they dropped
To bring the parson's son to aid.
Their cycling suits were tailor-made
Smart, mannish, pert, but feminine.
The colour and the zest of wine
Were in their presence and their bearing
Like spring, they brought the thought of pairing.
The parson's lady thought them pert.
And they could mock a man and flirt,
Do billiard tricks with corks and pennies,
Sing ragtime songs and win at tennis
The silver-cigarette-case-prize.
They had good colour and bright eyes,
Bright hair, bright teeth and pretty skin,
Which many lads had longed to win
On darkened stairways after dances.
Their reading was the last romances,
And they were dashing hockey players,
Men called them, 'Jill and Joan, the slayers.'
They were as bright as fresh sweet-peas.

Old Farmer Bennett followed these
Upon his big-boned savage black
Whose mule-teeth yellowed to bite back
Whatever came within his reach.
Old Bennett sat him like a leech
The grim old rider seemed to be
As hard about the mouth as he.

The beaters nudged each other's ribs
With 'There he goes, his bloody Nibs.
He come on Joe and Anty Cop,
And beat 'em with his hunting-crop
Like tho' they'd bin a sack of beans.
His pickers were a pack of queans
And Joe and Anty took a couple.
He caught 'em there, and banged 'em supple.
Women and men, he didn't care
(He'd kill 'em someday, if he dare)
He beat the whole four nearly dead.
"I'll learn 'ee rabbit in my shed

That's how my ricks get set afire."
That's what he said, the bloody liar;
Old oaf, I'd like to burn his ricks,
Th' old swine's too free with fists and sticks.
He keeps that Mrs. Jones himselve.'

Just like an axehead on its helve
Old Bennett sat and watched the gathering.
He'd given many a man a lathering
In field or barn, and women, too.
His cold eye searched the women through
With comment, and the men with scorn.
He hated women gently born,
He hated all beyond his grasp
For he was minded like the asp
That strikes whatever is not dust.

Charles Copse, of Copse Hold Manor, thrust
Next into view. In face and limb
The beauty and the grace of him
Were like the golden age returned.
His grave eyes steadily discerned
The good in men and what was wise.
He had deep blue, mild-coloured eyes
And shocks of harvest-coloured hair
Still beautiful with youth. An air
Or power of kindness went about him;
No heart of youth could ever doubt him
Or fail to follow where he led.
He was a genius, simply bred,
And quite unconscious of his power.
He was the very red rose flower
Of all that coloured countryside.
Gauchos had taught him how to ride.
He knew all arts, but practised most
The art of bettering flesh and ghost
In men and lads down in the mud.
He knew no class in flesh and blood.
He loved his kind. He spent some pith
Long since, relieving Ladysmith.
Many a horse he trotted tame
Heading commandos from their aim
In those old days upon the veldt.

An old bear in a scarlet pelt
Came next, old Squire Harridew,
His eyebrows gave a man the grue
So bushy and so fierce they were;
He had a bitter tongue to swear.
A fierce, hot, hard, old, stupid Squire,
With all his liver made of fire,
Small brain, great courage, mulish will.
The hearts in all his house stood still
When someone crossed the Squire's path.
For he was terrible in wrath,
And smashed whatever came to hand.
Two things he failed to understand,
The foreigner and what was new.

His daughters, Carrie, Jane and Lou
Rode with him, Carrie at his side.
His son, the ne'er-do-weel, had died
In Arizona, long before.
The Squire set the greatest store
By Carrie, youngest of the three,
And lovely to the blood was she;
Blonde, with a face of blush and cream,
And eyes deep violet in their gleam,
Bright blue when quiet in repose.
She was a very golden rose.
And many a man when sunset came
Would see the manor windows flame,
And think, 'My beauty's home is there.'
Queen Helen had less golden hair,
Queen Cleopatra paler lips,
Queen Blanche's eyes were in eclipse,
By golden Carrie's glancing by.
She had a wit for mockery
And sang mild, pretty senseless songs
Of sunsets, Heav'n and lover's wrongs,
Sweet to the Squire when he had dined.
A rosebud need not have a mind.
A lily is not sweet from learning.

Jane looked like a dark lantern, burning,
Outwardly dark, unkempt, uncouth,
But minded like the living truth,
A friend that nothing shook nor wearied

She was not 'Darling Jane'd,' nor 'Dearie'd,'
She was all prickles to the touch,
So sharp, that many feared to clutch,
So keen, that many thought her bitter.
She let the little sparrows twitter.
She had a hard ungracious way.
Her storm of hair was iron-grey,
And she was passionate in her heart
For women's souls that burn apart,
Just as her mother's had, with Squire.
She gave the sense of smouldering fire.
She was not happy being a maid,
At home, with Squire, but she stayed
Enduring life, however bleak,
To guard her sisters who were weak,
And force a life for them from Squire.
And she had roused and stood his fire
A hundred times, and earned his hate,
To win those two a better state.
Long years before the Canon's son
Had cared for her, but he had gone
To Klondyke, to the mines, for gold,
To find, in some strange way untold,
A foreign grave that no men knew.

No depth, nor beauty, was in Lou,
But charm and fun, for she was merry,
Round, sweet and little like a cherry,
With laughter like a robin's singing;
She was not kitten-like and clinging,
But pert and arch and fond of flirting,
In mocking ways that were not hurting,
And merry ways that women pardoned.
Not being married yet she gardened.
She loved sweet music; she would sing
Songs made before the German King
Made England German in her mind.
She sang 'My lady is unkind,'
'The Hunt is up,' and those sweet things
Which Thomas Campion set to strings
'Thrice toss,' and 'What,' and 'Where are now?'

The next to come was Major Howe
Driv'n in a dog-cart by a groom.

The testy Major was in fume
To find no hunter standing waiting;
The groom who drove him caught a rating,
The groom who had the horse in stable,
Was damned in half the tongues of Babel.
The Major being hot and heady
When horse or dinner was not ready.
He was a lean, tough, liverish fellow,
With pale blue eyes, (the whites pale yellow),
Moustache clipped toothbrush-wise, and jaws
Shaved bluish like old partridge claws.
When he had stripped his coat he made
A speckless presence for parade,
New pink, white cords, and glossy tops,
New gloves, the newest thing in crops,
Worn with an air that well-expressed
His sense that no-one else was dressed.

Quick trotting after Major Howe
Came Doctor Frome of Quickemshow,
A smiling silent man whose brain
Knew all of every secret pain
In every man and woman there.
Their inmost lives were all laid bare
To him, because he touched their lives
When strong emotions sharp as knives
Brought out what sort of soul each was.
As secret as the graveyard grass
He was, as he had need to be.
At some time he had had to see
Each person there sans clothes, sans mask,
Sans lying even, when to ask
Probed a tamed spirit into truth.

Richard, his son, a jolly youth
Rode with him, fresh from Thomas's,
As merry as a yearling is
In maytime in a clover patch.
He was a gallant chick to hatch
Big, brown and smiling, blithe and kind,
With all his father's love of mind
And greater force to give it act.
To see him when the scrum was packt,
Heave, playing forward, was a sight.

His tackling was the crowd's delight
In many a danger close to goal.
The pride in the three-quarter's soul
Dropped, like a wet rag, when he collared.
He was as steady as a bollard,
And gallant as a skysail yard,
He rode a chestnut mare which sparred.
In good St. Thomas' Hospital,
He was the crown imperial
Of all the scholars of his year.

The Harold lads, from Tencombe Weir,
Came all on foot in corduroys,
Poor widowed Mrs. Harold's boys,
Dick, Hal and Charles, whose father died.
(Will Masemore shot him in the side
By accident at Masemore Farm
A hazel knocked Will Masemore's arm
In getting through a hedge; his gun
Was not half-cocked, so it was done
And those three boys left fatherless.)
Their gaitered legs were in a mess
With good red mud from twenty ditches,
Hal's face was plastered like his breeches.
Dick chewed a twig of juniper.
They kept at distance from the stir
Their loss had made them lads apart.

Next came the Colways' pony cart
From Coln St. Evelyn's with the party.
Hugh Colway jovial, bold and hearty
And Polly Colway's brother, John
(Their horses had been both sent on)
And Polly Colway drove them there.
Poor pretty Polly Colway's hair.
The grey mare killed her at the brook
Down Seven Springs Mead at Water Hook
Just one month later, poor sweet woman.
Her brother was a rat-faced Roman
Lean, puckered, tight-skinned from the sea
Commander in the *Canace*
Able to drive a horse, or ship,
Or crew of men, without a whip
By will, as long as they could go.

His face would wrinkle, row on row,
From mouth to hair-roots when he laught.
He looked ahead as though his craft
Were with him still, in dangerous channels.
He and Hugh Colway tossed their flannels
Into the pony-cart and mounted.
Six foiled attempts the watchers counted
The horses being bickering things
That so much scarlet made like kings
Such sidling and such pawing and shifting.

When Hugh was up his mare went drifting
Sidelong and feeling with her heels
For horses' legs and poshay wheels
While lather creamed her neat clipt skin.
Hugh guessed her foibles with a grin.
He was a rich town-merchant's son,
A wise and kind man fond of fun
Who loved to have a troop of friends
At Coln St. Eves for all weekends
And troops of children in for tea.
He gloried in a Christmas Tree.
And Polly was his heart's best treasure,
And Polly was a golden pleasure
To everyone, to see or hear.

Poor Polly's dying struck him queer,
He was a darkened man thereafter,
Cowed silent, he would wince at laughter
And be so gentle it was strange
Even to see. Life loves to change.

Now Coln St. Evelyn's hearths are cold,
The shutters up, the hunters sold,
And green mould damps the locked front door.
But this was still a month before,
And Polly, golden in the chaise,
Still smiled, and there were golden days,
Still thirty days, for those dear lovers.

The Riddens came, from Ocle Covers,
Bill Ridden riding Stormalong,
(By Tempest out of Love-me-long)
A proper handful of a horse,

16

That nothing but the Aintree course
Could bring to terms, save Bill perhaps.
All sport, from bloody war to craps,
Came well to Bill, that big-mouthed smiler
They nicknamed him 'the mug-beguiler,'
For Billy lived too much with horses
In coper's yards and sharper's courses
To lack the sharper-coper streak.
He did not turn the other cheek,
When struck (as English Christians do)
He boxed like a Whitechapel Jew
And many a time his knuckles bled
Against a race-course-gipsy's head.
For 'hit him first and argue later,'
Was truth at Billy's Alma Mater,
Not love, not any bosh of love.
His hand was like a chamois glove
And riding was his chief delight.
He bred the chaser Chinese White
From Lilybud by Mandarin.
And when his mouth tucked corners in
And scent was high and hounds were going
He went across a field like snowing
And tackled anything that came.

His wife, Sal Ridden, was the same,
A loud, bold, blonde abundant mare
With white horse-teeth and stooks of hair
(Like polished brass) and such a manner
It flaunted from her like a banner.
Her father was Tom See the trainer,
She rode a lovely earth-disdainer
Which she and Billy wished to sell.

Behind them rode her daughter Bell,
A strange shy lovely girl whose face
Was sweet with thought and proud with race,
And bright with joy at riding there.
She was as good as blowing air
But shy and difficult to know.
The kittens in the barley-mow,
The setter's toothless puppies sprawling,
The blackbird in the apple, calling,
All knew her spirit more than we.

17

So delicate these maidens be
In loving lovely helpless things.

The Manor set, from Tencombe Rings,
Came, with two friends, a set of six.
Ed Manor with his cockerel chicks,
Nob, Cob and Bunny as they called them,
(God help the school or rule which galled them;
They carried head) and friends from town.
Ed Manor trained on Tencombe Down.
He once had been a famous bat,
He had that stroke, 'the Manor-pat,'
Which snicked the ball for three, past cover.
He once scored twenty in an over,
But now he cricketed no more.
He purpled in the face and swore
At all three sons, and trained, and told
Long tales of cricketing of old,
When he alone had saved his side.
Drink made it doubtful if he lied,
Drink purpled him, he could not face
The fences now, nor go the pace
He brought his friends to meet; no more.

His big son Nob, at whom he swore,
Swore back at him, for Nob was surly,
Tall, shifty, sullen-smiling, burly,
Quite fearless, built with such a jaw
That no man's rule could be his law
Nor any woman's son his master.
Boxing he relished. He could plaster
All those who boxed out Tencombe way.
A front tooth had been knocked away
Two days before, which put his mouth
A little to the east of south.
And put a venom in his laughter.

Cob was a lighter lad, but dafter,
Just past eighteen, while Nob was twenty.
Nob had no nerves but Cob had plenty
So Cobby went where Nobby led.
He had no brains inside his head,
Was fearless, just like Nob, but put
Some clog of folly round his foot,

Where Nob put will of force or fraud.
He spat aside and muttered Gawd
When vext; he took to whiskey kindly
And loved and followed Nobby blindly,
And rode as in the saddle born.

Bun looked upon the two with scorn.
He was the youngest, and was wise.
He, too, was fair, with sullen eyes,
He too (a year before) had had
A zest for going to the bad,
With Cob and Nob. He knew the joys
Of drinking with the stable-boys,
Or smoking while he filled his skin
With pints of Guinness dashed with gin
And Cobby yelled a bawdy ditty,
Or cutting Nobby for the kitty,
And damning peoples' eyes and guts
Or drawing evening-church for sluts
He knew them all and now was quit.

Sweet Polly Colway managed it.
And Bunny changed. He dropped his drink
(The pleasant pit's seductive brink)
He started working in the stable,
And well, for he was shrewd and able.
He left the doubtful female friends
Picked up at Evening-Service-ends,
He gave up cards and swore no more.
Nob called him, 'the Reforming Whore,'
'The Soul's Awakening,' or 'The Text,'
Nob being always coarse when vext.

Ed Manor's friends were Hawke and Sladd,
Old college friends, the last he had,
Rare horsemen, but their nerves were shaken
By all the whiskey they had taken.
Hawke's hand was trembling on his rein.
His eyes were dead-blue like a vein,
His peaked sad face was touched with breeding,
His querulous mind was quaint from reading,
His piping voice still quirked with fun.
Many a mad thing he had done,
Riding to hounds and going to races.

A glimmer of the gambler's graces,
Wit, courage, devil, touched his talk.

Sladd's big fat face was white as chalk,
His mind went wandering, swift yet solemn,
Twixt winning-post and betting-column,
The weights and forms and likely colts.
He said, 'This road is full of jolts.
I shall be seasick riding here.
O, damn last night with that liqueur.'

Len Stokes rode up on Peterkin;
He owned the Downs by Baydon Whin;
And grazed some thousand sheep; the boy
Grinned round at men with jolly joy
At being alive and being there.
His big round face and mop of hair
Shone, his great teeth shone in his grin.
The clean blood in his clear tanned skin
Ran merry, and his great voice mocked
His young friends present till they rocked.

Steer Harpit came from Rowell Hill,
A small, frail man, all heart and will,
A sailor as his voice betrayed.
He let his whip-thong droop and played
At snicking off the grass-blades with it.
John Hankerton, from Compton Lythitt,
Was there with Pity Hankerton,
And Mike, their good-for-little son,
Back, smiling, from his seventh job.
Joan Urch was there upon her cob.
Tom Sparsholt on his lanky grey.
John Restrop from Hope Goneaway
And Vaughan, the big black handsome devil,
Loose-lipped with song and wine and revel
All rosy from his morning tub.

The Godsdown tigress with her cub
(Lady and Tommy Crowmarsh) came.
The great eyes smouldered in the dame,
Wit glittered, too, which few men saw.
There was more beauty there than claw.
Tommy in bearing, horse and dress

Was black, fastidious, handsomeness,
Choice to his trimmed soul's fingertips.
Heredia's sonnets on his lips.
A line undrawn, a plate (not bitten),
A stone (uncut), a phrase (unwritten)
That would be perfect, made his mind.
A choice pull, from a rare print, signed,
Was Tommy. He collected plate,
(Old Sheffield) and he owned each state
Of all the Meryon Paris etchings.
Colonel Sir Button Budd of Fletchings
Was there; Long Robert Thrupp was there
(Three yards of him men said there were)
Long as the King of Prussia's fancy.
He rode the long-legged Necromancy,
A useless racehorse that could canter.
George Childrey with his jolly banter
Was there, Nick Childrey, too, come down
The night before from London town
To hunt and have his lungs blown clean.
The Ilsley set from Tuttocks Green
Was there, (old Henry Ilsley drove),
Carlotta Ilsley brought her love
A flop-jowled broker from the city.
Men pitied her, for she was pretty.

Some grooms and second horsemen mustered.
A lot of men on foot were clustered
Round the inn-door, all busy drinking,
One heard the kissing glasses clinking
In passage as the tray was brought.
Two terriers (which they had there) fought
There on the green, a loud, wild whirl.
Bell stopped them like a gallant girl.
The hens behind the tavern clucked.

Then on a horse which bit and bucked,
(The half-broke four-year-old Marauder),
Came Minton-Price of th' Afghan border,
Lean, puckered, yellowed, knotted, scarred,
Tough as a hide-rope twisted hard,
Tense tiger-sinew knit to bone.
Strange-wayed from having lived alone
With Kafir, Afghan and Beloosh

In stations frozen in the Koosh
Where nothing but the bullet sings.
His mind had conquered many things –
Painting, mechanics, physics, law,
White-hot, hand-beaten things to draw
Self-hammered from his own soul's stithy,
His speech was blacksmith-sparked and pithy.
Danger had been his brother bred;
The stones had often been his bed
In bickers with the border-thieves.

A chestnut mare with swerves and heaves
Came plunging, scattering all the crowd,
She tossed her head and laughed aloud
And bickered sideways past the meet.
From pricking ears to mincing feet
She was all tense with blood and quiver
You saw her clipt hide twitch and shiver
Over her netted cords of veins.
She carried Cothill, of the Sleins,
A tall, black, bright-eyed handsome lad.
Great power and great grace he had.
Men hoped the greatest things of him.
His grace made people think him slim
But he was muscled like a horse,
A sculptor would have wrought his torse
In bronze or marble for Apollo.
He loved to hurry like a swallow
For miles on miles of short-grassed sweet
Blue-harebelled downs where dewy feet
Of pure winds hurry ceaselessly,
He loved the downland like a sea,
The downland where the kestrels hover
The downland had him for a lover.

And every other thing he loved
In which a clean free spirit moved.

So beautiful, he was, so bright,
He looked to men like young delight
Gone courting April maidenhood,
That has the primrose in her blood,
He on his mincing lady mare.

22

Ock Gurney and Old Pete were there
Riding their bonny cobs and swearing,
Ock's wife had giv'n them both a fairing,
A horse-rosette, red, white and blue.
Their cheeks were brown as any brew
And every comer to the meet
Said, 'Hello, Ock' or, 'Morning, Pete
Be you a-going to a wedding?'
'Why, noa,' they said, 'we'm going a-bedding;
Now ben't us, uncle, ben't us, Ock?'

Pete Gurney was a lusty cock
Turned sixty-three, but bright and hale,
A dairy-farmer in the vale,
Much like a robin in the face,
Much character in little space
With little eyes like burning coal.
His mouth was like a slit or hole
In leather that was seamed and lined.
He had the russet-apple mind
That betters as the weather worsen.
He was a manly English person
Kind to the core, brave, merry, true;
One grief he had, a grief still new
That former Parson joined with Squire
In putting down the Playing Quire
In church, and putting organ in.
'Ah, boys, that was a pious din
That Quire was; a pious praise
The noise was that we used to raise.
I and my serpent, George with his'n
On Easter Day in "He Is Risen"
Or blessed Christmas in "Venite"
And how the trombone came in mighty
In Alleluias from the heart.
Pious, for each man played his part
Not like 'tis now.' Thus he, still sore
For changes forty years before
When all (that could) in time and tune
Blew trumpets to the newë moon.
He was a bachelor, from choice.
He and his nephew farmed the Boyce
Prime pastureland for thirty cows.
Ock's wife, Selina Jane, kept house
And jolly were the three together.

Ock had a face like summer weather
A broad red sun, split by a smile.
He mopped his forehead all the while
And said, 'By damn,' and 'Ben't us, Unk?'
His eyes were close and deeply sunk.
He cursed his hunter like a lover,
'Now blast your soul, my dear, give over.
Woa, now, my pretty, damn your eyes.'
Like Pete he was of middle size,
Dean-oak-like, stuggy, strong in shoulder.
He stood a wrestle like a boulder.
He had a back for pitching hay.
His singing voice was like a bay.
In talk he had a sideways spit,
Each minute, to refresh his wit.
He cracked Brazil nuts with his teeth.
He challenged Cobbett of the Heath
(Weight-lifting champion) once, but lost.
Hunting was what he loved the most
Next to his wife and Uncle Pete.
With beer to drink and cheese to eat
And rain in May to fill the grasses
This life was not a dream that passes
To Ock, but like the summer flower.

But now the clock had struck the hour
And round the corner, down the road
The bob-bob-bobbing serpent flowed
With three black knobs upon its spine;
Three bobbing black-caps in a line.
A glimpse of scarlet at the gap
Showed underneath each bobbing cap
And at the corner by the gate
One heard Tom Dansey give a rate,
'Hep, drop it, Jumper; have a care'
There came a growl, half-rate, half-swear
A spitting crack, a tuneful whimper
And sweet religion entered Jumper.

There was a general turn of faces,
The men and horses shifted places,
And round the corner came the hunt,
Those feathery things, the hounds, in front,
Intent, wise, dipping, trotting, straying,

24

Smiling at people, shoving, playing,
Nosing to children's faces, waving
Their feathery sterns, and all behaving,
One eye to Dansey on Maroon.
Their padding cat-feet beat a tune
And though they trotted up so quiet
Their noses brought them news of riot,
Wild smells of things with living blood,
Hot smells, against the grippers good,
Of weasel, rabbit, cat and hare,
Whose feet had been before them there,
Whose taint still tingled every breath;
But Dansey on Maroon was death,
So, though their noses roved, their feet
Larked and trit-trotted to the meet.

Bill Tall and Ell and Mirtie Key
(Aged fourteen years between the three)
Were flooded by them at the bend,
They thought their little lives would end;
The grave sweet eyes looked into theirs,
Cold noses came, and clean short hairs
And tails all crumpled up like ferns,
A sea of moving heads and sterns,
All round them, brushing coat and dress,
One paused, expecting a caress.
The children shrank into each other,
Shut eyes, clutched tight, and shouted, 'Mother'
With mouths wide open, catching tears.

Sharp Mrs. Tall allayed their fears,
'Err out the road, the dogs won't hurt 'ee.
There now, you've cried your faces dirty.
More cleaning up for me to do.
What? Cry at dogs, great lumps like you?'
She licked her handkerchief and smeared
Their faces where the dirt appeared.

The hunt trit-trotted to the meeting,
Tom Dansey touching cap to greeting,
Slow-lifting crop-thong to the rim,
No hunter there got more from him,
Except some brightening of the eye.
He halted at the Cock and Pye,

The hounds drew round him on the green,
Arrogant, Daffodil and Queen,
Closest, but all in little space.
Some lolled their tongues, some made grimace,
Yawning, or tilting nose in quest,
All stood and looked about with zest,
They were uneasy as they waited.
Their sires and dams had been well-mated,
They were a lovely pack for looks;
Their forelegs drumsticked without crooks,
Straight, without over-tread or bend,
Muscled to gallop to the end,
With neat feet round as any cat's.
Great-chested, muscled in the slats,
Bright, clean, short-coated, broad in shoulder
With stag-like eyes that seemed to smoulder.
The heads well-cocked, the clean necks strong;
Brows broad, ears close, the muzzles long;
And all like racers in the thighs;
Their noses exquisitely wise,
Their minds being memories of smells;
Their voices like a ring of bells;
Their sterns all spirit, cock and feather;
Their colours like the English weather,
Magpie and hare- and badger-pye,
Like minglings in a double dye,
Some smutty-nosed, some tan, none bald;
Their manners were to come when called,
Their flesh was sinew knit to bone,
Their courage like a banner blown.
Their joy, to push him out of cover,
And hunt him till they rolled him over.
They were as game as Robert Dover.

Tom Dansey was a famous whip
Trained as a child in horsemanship
Entered, as soon as he was able
As boy at Caunter's racing-stable;
There, like the other boys, he slept
In stall beside the horse he kept,
Snug in the straw; and Caunter's stick
Brought morning to him all too quick.
He learned the high, quick gingery ways
Of thoroughbreds; his stable days

Made him a rider, groom and vet.
He promised to be too thickset
For jockeying, so left it soon.
Now he was whip and rode Maroon.
He was a small, lean, wiry man
With sunk cheeks weathered to a tan
Scarred by the spikes of hawthorn sprays
Dashed thro', head down, on going days,
In haste to see the line they took.
There was a beauty in his look,
It was intent. His speech was plain.
Maroon's head, reaching to the rein,
Had half his thought before he spoke.
His 'Gone Away,' when foxes broke
Was like a bell. His chief delight
Was hunting fox from noon to night.
His pleasure lay in hounds and horses;
He loved the Seven Springs water-courses
Those flashing brooks (in good sound grass,
Where scent would hang like breath on glass).
He loved the English countryside;
The wine-leaved bramble in the ride,
The lichen on the apple-trees,
The poultry ranging on the lees,
The farms, the moist earth-smelling cover,
His wife's green grave at Mitcheldover,
Where snowdrops pushed at the first thaw.
Under his hide his heart was raw
With joy and pity of these things.

The second whip was Kitty Myngs
Still but a lad but keen and quick
(Son of old Myngs who farmed the Wick)
A horse-mouthed lad who knew his work.
He rode the big black horse, the Turk,
And longed to be a huntsman bold.
He had the horse-look, sharp and old,
With much good-nature in his face.
His passion was to go the pace,
His blood was crying for a taming.
He was the Devil's chick for gaming,
He was a rare good lad to box.
He sometimes had a main of cocks
Down at the Flags. His job with hounds

At present kept his blood in bounds
From rioting and running hare.
Tom Dansey made him have a care.
He worshipped Dansey heart and soul.
To be a huntsman was his goal;
To be with hounds, to charge full tilt
Blackthorns that made the gentry wilt
Was his ambition and his hope.
He was a hot colt needing rope.
He was too quick to speak his passion
To suit his present huntsman's fashion.

The huntsman, Robin Dawe, looked round,
He sometimes called a favourite hound,
Gently, to see the creature turn
Look happy up and wag his stern.
He smiled and nodded and saluted
To those who hailed him, as it suited.
And patted Pip's, his hunter's neck.
His new pink was without a speck.
He was a red-faced smiling fellow,
His voice clear tenor, full and mellow,
His eyes, all fire, were black and small.
He had been smashed in many a fall.
His eyebrow had a white curved mark
Left by the bright shoe of The Lark
Down in a ditch by Seven Springs.
His coat had all been trod to strings,
His ribs laid bare and shoulder broken
Being jumped on down at Water's Oaken
The time his horse came down and rolled.
His face was of the country mould
Such as the mason sometimes cutted
On English moulding-ends which jutted
Out of the church walls, centuries since.
And as you never know the quince,
How good he is, until you try,
So, in Dawe's face, what met the eye
Was only part, what lay behind
Was English character and mind.
Great kindness, delicate sweet feeling,
(Most shy, most clever in concealing
Its depth) for beauty of all sorts,
Great manliness and love of sports,

A grave, wise thoughtfulness and truth,
A merry fun, outlasting youth,
A courage terrible to see
And mercy for his enemy.

He had a clean-shaved face, but kept
A hedge of whisker neatly clipt,
A narrow strip or picture frame,
(Old Dawe, the woodman, did the same),
Under his chin from ear to ear.

But now the resting hounds gave cheer,
Joyful and Arrogant and Catch-him,
Smelt the glad news and ran to snatch him,
The Master's dogcart turned the bend.
Damsel and Skylark knew their friend,
A thrill ran through the pack like fire
And little whimpers ran in quire.
The horses cocked and pawed and whickered,
Young Cothill's chaser kicked and bickered
And stood on end and struck out sparks.
Joyful and Catch-him sang like larks.
There was the Master in the trap,
Clutching Old Roman in his lap,
Old Roman, crazy for his brothers,
And putting frenzy in the others,
To set them at the dogcart wheels,
With thrusting heads and little squeals.

The Master put Old Roman by,
And eyed the thrusters heedfully,
He called a few pet hounds and fed
Three special friends with scraps of bread,
Then peeled his wraps, climbed down and strode
Through all those clamourers in the road,
Saluted friends, looked round the crowd,
Saw Harridew's three girls and bowed,
Then took White Rabbit from the groom.

He was Sir Peter Bynd, of Coombe;
Past sixty now, though hearty still,
A living picture of good-will,
An old, grave soldier, sweet and kind,
A courtier with a knightly mind,

Who felt whatever thing he thought.
His face was scarred, for he had fought
Five wars for us. Within his face
Courage and power had their place,
Rough energy, decision, force.
He smiled about him from his horse.
He had a welcome and salute
For all, on horse or wheel or foot,
Whatever kind of life each followed.
His tanned, drawn cheeks looked old and hollowed,
But still his bright blue eyes were young,
And when the pack crashed into tongue,
And staunch White Rabbit shook like fire,
He sent him at it like a flier,
And lived with hounds while horses could.

'They'm lying in the Ghost Heath Wood,
Sir Peter,' said an earth-stopper,
(Old Baldy Hill), 'You'll find 'em there.
'Z I come'd across I smell 'em plain.
There's one up back, down Tuttock's drain,
But, Lord, it's just a bog, the Tuttocks,
Hounds would be swallered to the buttocks.
Heath Wood, Sir Peter, 's best to draw.'

Sir Peter gave two minutes' law
For Kingston Challow and his daughter;
He said, 'They're late. We'll start the slaughter.
Ghost Heath, then, Dansey. We'll be going.'

Now, at his word, the tide was flowing.
Off went Maroon, off went the hounds,
Down road, then off, to Chols Elm Grounds,
Across soft turf with dead leaves cleaving
And hillocks that the mole was heaving,
Mild going to those trotting feet.
After the scarlet coats, the meet
Came clopping up the grass in spate
They poached the trickle at the gate
Their horses' feet sucked at the mud,
Excitement in the horses' blood
Cocked forward every ear and eye;
They quivered as the hounds went by,
They trembled when they first trod grass;

They would not let another pass,
They scattered wide up Chols Elm Hill.

The wind was westerly but still,
The sky a high fair-weather cloud,
Like meadows ridge-and-furrow ploughed,
Just glinting sun but scarcely moving.
Blackbirds and thrushes thought of loving,
Catkins were out; the day seemed tense
It was so still. At every fence
Cow-parsley pushed its thin green fern.
White-violet-leaves shewed at the burn.

Young Cothill let his chaser go
Round Chols Elm Field a turn or so
To soothe his edge. The riders went
Chatting and laughing and content
In groups of two or three together.
The hounds, a flock of shaking feather
Bobbed on ahead, past Chols Elm Cop,
The horses' shoes went clip-a-clop,
Along the stony cart-track there,
The little spinney was all bare,
But in the earth-moist winter day
The scarlet coats twixt tree and spray,
The glistening horses pressing on,
The brown-faced lads, Bill, Dick and John,
And all the hurry to arrive
Were beautiful like spring alive.

The hounds melted away with Master
The tanned lads ran, the field rode faster,
The chatter joggled in the throats
Of riders bumping by like boats,
'We really ought to hunt a bye day.'
'Fine day for scent,' 'A fly or die day.'
'They chopped a bagman in the check,
He had a collar round his neck.'
'Old Ridden's girl's a pretty flapper.'
'That Vaughan's a cad, the whippersnapper.'
'I tell 'ee, lads, I seed 'em plain
Down in the Rough at Shifford's Main,
Old Squire stamping like a Duke
So red with blood I thought he'd puke

In appleplexie, as they do.
Miss Jane stood just as white as dew
And heard him out in just white heat
And then she trimmed him down a treat
About Miss Lou it was, or Carrie
(She'd be a pretty peach to marry).'

'Her'll draw up-wind, so us'll go
Down by the furze, we'll see 'em so.'
'Look, there they go, lad.'

               There they went,
Across the brook and up the bent,
Past Primrose Wood, past Brady Ride,
Along Ghost Heath to cover side.
The bobbing scarlet, trotting pack,
Turf scatters tossed behind each back,
Some horses blowing with a whinny,
A jam of horses in the spinney,
Close to the ride-gate; leather straining,
Saddles all creaking; men complaining,
Chaffing each other as they pass't.
On Ghost Heath turf they trotted fast.

Now as they neared the Ghost Heath Wood,
Some riders grumbled, 'What's the good?
It's shot all day and poached all night.
We shall draw blank and lose the light,
And lose the scent, and lose the day.
Why can't he draw Hope Goneaway,
Or Tuttocks Wood, instead of this?
There's no fox here, there never is.'

But as he trotted up to cover
Robin was watching to discover
What chance there was, and many a token
Told him that though no hound had spoken,
Most of them stirred to something there.
The old hounds' muzzles searched the air,
Thin ghosts of scents were in their teeth,
From foxes which had crossed the Heath,
Not very many hours before.
'We'll find,' he said, 'I'll bet, a score.'

Along Ghost Heath they trotted well,
The hoof-cuts made the bruised earth smell,
The shaken brambles scattered drops,
Stray pheasants kukkered out of copse,
Cracking the twigs down with their knockings
And planing out of sight with cockings;
A scut or two lopped white to bramble.

And now they gathered to the gamble
At Ghost Heath Wood on Ghost Heath Down,
The hounds went crackling through the brown
Dry stalks of bracken killed by frost.
The wood stood silent in its host
Of halted trees all winter bare.
The boughs, like veins that suck the air,
Stretched tense, the last leaf scarcely stirred.
There came no song from any bird;
The darkness of the wood stood still
Waiting for fate on Ghost Heath Hill.

The whips crept to the sides to view,
The Master gave the nod, and 'Leu,
Leu in, Ed-Hoick, Ed-Hoick, Leu in,'
Went Robin, cracking through the whin
And through the hedge-gap into cover.
The binders crashed as hounds went over,
And cock-cock-cock the pheasants rose.
Then up went stern and down went nose,
And Robin's cheerful tenor cried,
Through hazel-scrub and stub and ride
'O wind him beauties, push him out,
Yooi, onto him, Yahout, Yahout,
O, push him out, Yooi, wind him, wind him.'
The beauties burst the scrub to find him,
They nosed the warren's clipped green lawn
The bramble and the broom were drawn,
The covert's northern end was blank.

They turned to draw along the bank
Through thicker cover than the Rough
Through three-and-four-year understuff
Where Robin's forearm screened his eyes
'Yooi, find him, beauties,' came his cries
'Hark, hark to Daffodil,' the laughter

Fal'n from his horn, brought whimpers after,
For ends of scents were everywhere.
He said, 'This Hope's a likely lair.
And there's his billets, gray and furred.
And George, he's moving, there's a bird.'

A blue uneasy jay was chacking
(A swearing screech, like tearing sacking)
From tree to tree, as in pursuit,
He said, 'That's it. There's fox afoot.
And there, they're feathering, there she speaks.
Good Daffodil, good Tarrybreeks,
Hark there, to Daffodil, hark, hark.'
The mild horn's note, the soft flaked spark
Of music, fell on that rank scent.
From heart to wild heart magic went.
The whimpering quivered, quavered, rose.
'Daffodil has it, there she goes.
O hark to her.' With wild high crying
From frantic hearts, the hounds went flying
To Daffodil, for that rank taint.
A waft of it came warm but faint
In Robin's mouth, and faded so.
'First find a fox, then let him go,'
Cried Robin Dawe. 'For any sake.
Ring, Charley, till you're fit to break.'
He cheered his beauties like a lover
And charged beside them into cover.

Part II

On old Cold Crendon's windy tops
Grows wintrily Blown Hilcote Copse,
Wind-bitten beech with badger barrows,
Where brocks eat wasp-grubs with their marrows,
And foxes lie on short-grassed turf,
Nose between paws, to hear the surf
Of wind in the beeches drowsily.
There was our fox bred lustily
Three years before, and there he berthed
Under the beech-roots snugly earthed,
With a roof of flint and a floor of chalk,
And ten bitten hens' heads each on its stalk,
Some rabbits' paws, some fur from scuts,
A badger's corpse and a smell of guts.
And there on the night before my tale
He trotted out for a point in the vale.

He saw, from the cover edge, the valley
Go trooping down with its droops of sally
To the brimming river's lipping bend
And a light in the inn at Water's End.
He heard the owl go hunting by
And the shriek of the mouse the owl made die,
And the purr of the owl as he tore the red
Strings from between his claws and fed;
The smack of joy of the horny lips
Marbled green with the blobby strips.
He saw the farms where the dogs were barking,
Cold Crendon Court and Copsecote Larking;
The fault with the spring as bright as gleed,
Green-slash-laced with water-weed.
A glare in the sky still marked the town,
Though all folk slept and the blinds were down,
The street lamps watched the empty square,
The night-cat sang his evil there.

The fox's nose tipped up and round
Since smell is a part of sight and sound.
Delicate smells were drifting by,

The sharp nose flaired them heedfully;
Partridges in the clover stubble,
Crouched in a ring for the stoat to nubble.
Rabbit bucks beginning to box;
A scratching place for the pheasant cocks;
A hare in the dead grass near the drain,
And another smell like the spring again.

A faint rank taint like April coming,
It cocked his ears and his blood went drumming,
For somewhere out by Ghost Heath Stubs
Was a roving vixen wanting cubs.
Over the valley, floating faint
On a warmth of windflow came the taint,
He cocked his ears, he upped his brush,
And he went up wind like an April thrush.

By the Roman Road to Braiches Ridge
Where the fallen willow makes a bridge,
Over the brook by White Hart's Thorn,
To the acres thin with pricking corn,
Over the sparse green hair of the wheat,
By the Clench Brook Mill at Clench Brook Leat,
Through Cowfoot Pastures to Nonely Stevens,
And away to Poltrewood St. Jevons.
Past Tott Hill Down all snaked with meuses,
Past Clench St. Michael and Naunton Crucis,
Past Howle's Oak Farm where the raving brain
Of a dog who heard him foamed his chain,
Then off, as the farmer's window opened,
Past Stonepits Farm to Upton Hope End,
Over short sweet grass and worn flint arrows
And the three dumb hows of Tencombe Barrows.
And away and away with a rolling scramble,
Through the blackthorn and up the bramble,
With a nose for the smells the night wind carried,
And his red fell clean for being married,
For clicketting time and Ghost Heath Wood,
Had put the violet in his blood.

At Tencombe Rings near the Manor Linney,
His foot made the great black stallion whinny,
And the stallion's whinny aroused the stable
And the bloodhound bitches stretched their cable,

And the clink of the bloodhounds' chain aroused
The sweet-breathed kye as they chewed and drowsed
And the stir of the cattle changed the dream
Of the cat in the loft to tense green gleam.
The red-wattled black cock hot from Spain
Crowed from his perch for dawn again,
His breast-pufft hens, one-legged on perch,
Gurgled, beak-down, like men in church,
They crooned in the dark, lifting one red eye
In the raftered roost as the fox went by.

By Tencombe Regis and Slaughters Court,
Through the great grass square of Roman Fort,
By Nun's Wood Yews and the Hungry Hill,
And the Corpse Way Stones all standing still,
By Seven Springs Mead to Deerlip Brook,
And a lolloping leap to Water Hook.
Then with eyes like sparks and his blood awoken
Over the grass to Water's Oaken,
And over the hedge and into ride
In Ghost Heath Wood for his roving bride.

Before the dawn he had loved and fed
And found a kennel and gone to bed
On a shelf of grass in a thick of gorse
That would bleed a hound and blind a horse.
There he slept in the mild west weather
With his nose and brush well tuckt together,
He slept like a child, who sleeps yet hears
With the self who needs neither eyes nor ears.

He slept while the pheasant cock untucked
His head from his wing, flew down and kukked,
While the drove of the starlings whirred and wheeled
Out of the ash-trees into field.
While with great black flags that flogged and paddled
The rooks went out to the plough and straddled,
Straddled wide on the moist red cheese,
Of the furrows driven at Uppat's Leas.

Down in the village, men awoke,
The chimneys breathed with a faint blue smoke,
The fox slept on, though tweaks and twitches
Due to his dreams, ran down his flitches.

The cows were milked and the yards were sluict,
And the cocks and hens let out of roost,
Windows were opened, mats were beaten,
All men's breakfasts were cooked and eaten,
But out in the gorse on the grassy shelf,
The sleeping fox looked after himself.

Deep in his dream he heard the life
Of the woodland seek for food or wife,
The hop of a stoat, a buck that thumped,
The squeal of a rat as a weasel jumped,
The blackbird's chackering scattering crying,
The rustling bents from the rabbits flying,
Cows in a byre, and distant men,
And Condicote church-clock striking ten.

At eleven o'clock a boy went past,
With a rough-haired terrier following fast
The boy's sweet whistle and dog's quick yap
Woke the fox from out of his nap.

He rose and stretched till the claws in his pads,
Stuck hornily out like long black gads,
He listened a while, and his nose went round
To catch the smell of the distant sound.

The windward smells came free from taint
They were rabbit, strongly, with lime-kiln, faint,
A wild-duck, likely, at Sars Holt Pond,
And sheep on the Sars Holt Down beyond.

The lee-ward smells were much less certain
For the Ghost Heath Hill was like a curtain,
Yet vague, from the lee-ward, now and then,
Came muffled sounds like the sound of men.

He moved to his right to a clearer space,
And all his soul came into his face,
Into his eyes and into his nose,
As over the hill a murmur rose.
His ears were cocked and his keen nose flaired,
He sneered with his lips till his teeth were bared,
He trotted right and lifted a pad
Trying to test what foes he had.

On Ghost Heath turf was a steady drumming
Which sounded like horses quickly coming,
It died as the hunt went down the dip,
Then Malapert yelped at Myngs' whip.
A bright iron horseshoe clinkt on stone,
Then a man's voice spoke, not one alone,
Then a burst of laughter, swiftly still,
Muffled away by Ghost Heath Hill.
Then, indistinctly, the clop-clip-clep
On Brady Ride, of a horse's step,
Then silence, then, in a burst, much clearer,
Voices and horses coming nearer,
And another noise, of a pit-pat-beat
On the Ghost Hill grass, of fox-hound feet.

He sat on his haunches listening hard,
While his mind went over the compass card,
Men were coming and rest was done,
But he still had time to get fit to run;
He could outlast horse and outrace hound,
But men were devils from Lobs' Pound.
Scent was burning, the going good,
The world one lust for a fox's blood,
The main earths stopped and the drains put to,
And fifteen miles to the land he knew.
But of all the ills, the ill least pleasant
Was to run in the light when men were present.
Men in the fields to shout and sign
For a lift of hounds to a fox's line.
Men at the earth at the long point's end,
Men at each check and none his friend,
Guessing each shift that a fox contrives:–
But still, needs must when the devil drives.

He readied himself, then a soft horn blew,
Then a clear voice carolled, 'Ed-Hoick. Eleu.'
Then the wood-end rang with the clear voice crying,
And the crackle of scrub where hounds were trying.
Then the horn blew nearer, a hound's voice quivered,
Then another, then more, till his body shivered,
He left his kennel and trotted thence
With his ears flexed back and his nerves all tense.

He trotted down with his nose intent
For a fox's line to cross his scent,
It was only fair (he being a stranger)
That the native fox should have the danger.
Danger was coming, so swift, so swift,
That the pace of his trot began to lift
The blue-winged Judas, a jay, began
Swearing, hounds whimpered, air stank of man.

He hurried his trotting, he now felt frighted,
It was his poor body made hounds excited.
He felt as he ringed the great wood through
That he ought to make for the land he knew.

Then the hounds' excitement quivered and quickened
Then a horn blew death till his marrow sickened
Then the wood behind was a crash of cry
For the blood in his veins; it made him fly.

They were on his line; it was death to stay
He must make for home by the shortest way
But with all this yelling and all this wrath
And all these devils, how find a path?

He ran like a stag to the wood's north corner,
Where the hedge was thick and the ditch a yawner,
But the scarlet glimpse of Myngs on Turk,
Watching the woodside, made him shirk.

He ringed the wood and looked at the south.
What wind there was blew into his mouth.
But close to the woodland's blackthorn thicket
Was Dansey, still as a stone, on Picket.
At Dansey's back were a twenty more
Watching the cover and pressing fore.

The fox drew in and flaired with his muzzle.
Death was there if he messed the puzzle.
There were men without and hounds within,
A crying that stiffened the hair on skin,
Teeth in cover and death without,
Both deaths coming, and no way out.

His nose ranged swiftly, his heart beat fast,
Then a crashing cry rose up in a blast
Then horse hooves trampled, then horses' flitches
Burst their way through the hazel switches
Then the horn again made the hounds like mad
And a man, quite near, said, 'Found, by Gad,'
And a man, quite near, said, 'Now he'll break.
Lark's Leybourne Copse is the line he'll take.'
And the men moved up with their talk and stink
And the traplike noise of the horseshoe clink.
Men whose coming meant death from teeth
In a worrying wrench with him beneath.

The fox sneaked down by the cover side,
(With his ears flexed back) as a snake would glide
He took the ditch at the cover-end,
He hugged the ditch as his only friend.
The blackbird cock with the golden beak
Got out of his way with a jabbering shriek
And the shriek told Tom on the raking bay
That for eighteen pence he was gone away.

He ran in the hedge in the triple growth
Of bramble and hawthorn, glad of both,
Till a couple of fields were past, and then
Came the living death of the dread of men.

Then, as he listened, he heard a 'Hoy,'
Tom Dansey's horn and 'Awa-wa-woy.'
Then all hounds crying with all their forces
Then a thundering down of seventy horses.
Robin Dawe's horn and halloos of 'Hey
Hark Hollar, Hoik' and 'Gone Away,'
'Hark Hollar Hoik,' and the smack of a whip
A yelp as a tail hound caught the clip.
'Hark Hollar, Hark Hollar;' then Robin made
Pip go crash through the cut and laid,
Hounds were over and on his line
With a head like bees upon Tipple Tine.
The sound of the nearness sent a flood
Of terror of death through the fox's blood.
He upped his brush and he cocked his nose,
And he went upwind as a racer goes.

Bold Robin Dawe was over first,
Cheering his hounds on at the burst;
The field were spurring to be in it
'Hold hard, sirs, give them half a minute'
Came from Sir Peter on his white.
The hounds went romping with delight
Over the grass and got together;
The tail hounds galloped hell-for-leather
After the pack at Myngs' yell;
A cry like every kind of bell
Rang from these rompers as they raced.

The riders thrusting to be placed
Jammed down their hats and shook their horses,
The hounds romped past with all their forces,
They crashed into the blackthorn fence;
The scent was heavy on their sense,
So hot it seemed the living thing
It made the blood within them sing;
Gusts of it made their hackles rise,
Hot gulps of it were agonies
Of joy, and thirst for blood, and passion.
'Forrard,' cried Robin, 'that's the fashion.'
He raced beside his pack to cheer.
The field's noise died upon his ear,
A faint horn, far behind, blew thin
In cover, lest some hound were in.
Then instantly the great grass rise
Shut field and cover from his eyes
He and his racers were alone.
'A dead fox or a broken bone'
Said Robin, peering for his prey.

The rise, which shut his field away,
Shewed him the vale's great map spread out,
The downs' lean flank and thrusting snout,
Pale pastures, red-brown plough, dark wood,
Blue distance, still as solitude,
Glitter of water here and there,
The trees so delicately bare.
The dark green gorse and bright green holly.
'O glorious God,' he said, 'how jolly.'
And there, down hill, two fields ahead
The lolloping red dog-fox sped

Over Poor Pastures to the brook.
He grasped these things in one swift look
Then dived into the bullfinch heart
Through thorns that ripped his sleeves apart
And skutched new blood upon his brow.
'His point's Lark's Leybourne Covers now,'
Said Robin, landing with a grunt,
'Forrard, my beautifuls.'

               The hunt
Followed downhill to race with him,
White Rabbit with his swallow's skim,
Drew within hail, 'Quick burst, Sir Peter.'
'A traveller. Nothing could be neater.
Making for Godsdown Clumps, I take it?'
'Lark's Leybourne, sir, if he can make it.
Forrard.'

            Bill Ridden thundered down,
His big mouth grinned beneath his frown,
The hounds were going away from horses.
He saw the glint of watercourses,
Yell Brook and Wittold's Dyke ahead,
His horseshoes sliced the green turf red.
Young Cothill's chaser rushed and passt him,
Nob Manor, running next, said 'Blast him.
That poet chap who thinks he rides.'
Hugh Colway's mare made straking strides
Across the grass, the Colonel next;
Then Squire, volleying oaths and vext,
Fighting his hunter for refusing;
Bell Ridden like a cutter cruising,
Sailing the grass, then Cob on Warder,
Then Minton Price upon Marauder;
Ock Gurney with his eyes intense,
Burning as with a different sense,
His big mouth muttering glad 'By Damns;'
Then Pete crouched down from head to hams,
Rapt like a saint, bright focussed flame;
Bennett with devils in his wame
Chewing black cud and spitting slanting;
Copse scattering jests and Stukeley ranting;
Sal Ridden taking line from Dansey;
Long Robert forcing Necromancy;

A dozen more with bad beginnings;
Myngs riding hard to snatch an innings,
A wild last hound with high shrill yelps,
Smacked forrard with some whip-thong skelps.
Then last of all, at top of rise,
The crowd on foot all gasps and eyes;
The run up hill had winded them.

They saw the Yell Brook like a gem
Blue in the grass a short mile on
They heard faint cries, but hounds were gone
A good eight fields and out of sight
Except a rippled glimmer white
Going away with dying cheering
And scarlet flappings disappearing,
And scattering horses going, going,
Going like mad, White Rabbit snowing
Far on ahead, a loose horse taking
Fence after fence with stirrups shaking,
And scarlet specks and dark specks dwindling.

Nearer, were twigs knocked into kindling,
A much bashed fence still dropping stick,
Flung clods, still quivering from the kick,
Cut hoof-marks pale in cheesy clay,
The horse-smell blowing clean away,
Birds flitting back into the cover.
One last, faint cry, then all was over.
The hunt had been, and found, and gone.

At Neakings Farm, three furlongs on,
Hounds raced across the Waysmore Road,
Where many of the riders slowed
To tittup down a grassy lane
Which led as hounds led in the main
And gave no danger of a fall.
There, as they tittupped one and all,
Big Twenty Stone came scattering by,
His great mare made the hoof-casts fly.
'By leave,' he cried, 'Come on. Come up.
This fox is running like a tup;
Let's leave this lane and get to terms.
No sense in crawling here like worms.
Come let me past and let me start.

This fox is running like a hart,
And this is going to be a run.
Come on. I want to see the fun.
Thanky. By leave. Now, Maiden; do it.'
He faced the fence and put her through it
Shielding his eyes lest spikes should blind him,
The crashing blackthorn closed behind him.
Mud-scatters chased him as he scudded.
His mare's ears cocked, her neat feet thudded.

The kestrel cruising over meadow
Watched the hunt gallop on his shadow,
Wee figures, almost at a stand,
Crossing the multi-coloured land,
Slow as a shadow on a dial.

Some horses, swerving at a trial,
Baulked at a fence: at gates they bunched.
The mud about the gates was dunched
Like German cheese; men pushed for places,
And kicked the mud into the faces
Of those who made them room to pass.
The half-mile's gallop on the grass
Had tailed them out, and warmed their blood.
'His point's the Banner Barton Wood.'
'That, or Goat's Gorse.' 'A stinger, this.'
'You're right in that; by Jove it is.'
'An up-wind travelling fox, by George.'
'They say Tom viewed him at the forge.'
'Well, let me pass and let's be on.'

They crossed the lane to Tolderton,
The hill-marl died to valley clay,
And there before them ran the grey
Yell Water, swirling as it ran,
The Yell Brook of the hunting man.
The hunters eyed it and were grim.

They saw the water snaking slim
Ahead, like silver; they could see
(Each man) his pollard willow tree
Firming the bank, they felt their horses
Catch the gleam's hint and gather forces;
They heard the men behind draw near.

Each horse was trembling as a spear
Trembles in hand when tense to hurl,
They saw the brimmed brook's eddies curl,
The willow-roots like water-snakes;
The beaten holes the ratten makes,
They heard the water's rush; they heard
Hugh Colway's mare come like a bird;
A faint cry from the hounds ahead
Then saddle-strain, the bright hooves' tread,
Quick words, the splash of mud, the launch,
The sick hope that the bank be staunch,
Then Souse, with Souse to left and right.
Maroon across, Sir Peter's White
Down but pulled up, Tom over, Hugh
Mud to the hat but over, too,
Well splashed by Squire who was in.

With draggled pink stuck close to skin
The Squire leaned from bank and hauled
His mired horse's rein; he bawled
For help from each man racing by.
'What, help you pull him out? Not I.
What made you pull him in?' They said.
Nob Manor cleared and turned his head,
And cried 'Wade up. The ford's up-stream.'
Ock Gurney in a cloud of steam
Stood by his dripping cob and wrung
The taste of brook mud from his tongue
And scraped his poor cob's pasterns clean.
'Lord, what a crowner we've a-been,
This jumping brook's a mucky job.'
He muttered, grinning, 'Lord, poor cob.
Now, sir, let me.' He turned to Squire
And cleared his hunter from the mire
By skill and sense and strength of arm.

Meanwhile the fox passed Nonesuch Farm,
Keeping the spinney on his right.
Hounds raced him here with all their might
Along the short firm grass, like fire.
The cowman viewed him from the byre
Lolloping on, six fields ahead,
Then hounds, still carrying such a head,
It made him stare, then Rob on Pip,

46

Sailing the great grass like a ship,
Then grand Maroon in all his glory
Sweeping his strides, his great chest hoary
With foam fleck and the pale hill-marl.
They strode the Leet, they flew the Snarl,
They knocked the nuts at Nonesuch Mill,
Raced up the spur of Gallows Hill
And viewed him there. The line he took
Was Tineton and the Pantry Brook,
Going like fun and hounds like mad.
Tom glanced to see what friends he had
Still within sight, before he turned
The ridge's shoulder; he discerned,
One field away, young Cothill sailing
Easily up, Pete Gurney failing,
Hugh Colway quartering on Sir Peter,
Bill waiting on the mare to beat her,
Sal Ridden skirting to the right.
A horse, with stirrups flashing bright
Over his head at every stride,
Looked like the Major's; Tom espied
Far back, a scarlet speck of man
Running, and straddling as he ran.
Charles Copse was up, Nob Manor followed,
Then Bennett's big-boned black that wallowed,
Clumsy, but with the strength of ten.
Then black and brown and scarlet men,
Brown horses, white and black and grey
Scattered a dozen fields away.
The shoulder shut the scene away.

From the Gallows Hill to the Tineton Copse
There were ten ploughed fields like ten full stops,
All wet red clay where a horse's foot
Would be swathed, feet thick, like an ash-tree root.
The fox raced on, on the headlands firm,
Where his swift feet scared the coupling worm,
The rooks rose raving to curse him raw,
He snarled a sneer at their swoop and caw.
Then on, then on, down a half-ploughed field
Where a ship-like plough drove glitter-keeled,
With a bay horse near and a white horse leading,
And a man saying 'Zook' and the red earth bleeding.
He gasped as he saw the ploughman drop
The stilts and swear at the team to stop.
The ploughman ran in his red clay clogs
Crying, 'Zick-un, Towzer; Zick, good dogs.'
A couple of wire-haired lurchers lean
Arose from his wallet, nosing keen;
With a rushing swoop they were on his track,
Putting chest to stubble to bite his back.
He swerved from his line with the curs at heel,
The teeth as they missed him clicked like steel,
With a worrying snarl, they quartered on him,
While the ploughman shouted, 'Zick; upon him.'

The lurcher dogs soon shot their bolt,
And the fox raced on by the Hazel Holt,
Down the dead grass tilt to the sandstone gash
Of the Pantry Brook at Tineton Ash.
The loitering water, flooded full,
Had yeast on its lip like raddled wool,
It was wrinkled over with Arab script
Of eddies that twisted up and slipt.
The stepping stones had a rush about them
So the fox plunged in and swam without them.

He crossed to the cattle's drinking shallow
Firmed up with rush and the roots of mallow,
He wrung his coat from his draggled bones
And romped away for the Sarsen Stones.

A sneaking glance with his ears flexed back,
Made sure that his scent had failed the pack,
For the red clay, good for corn and roses,
Was cold for scent and brought hounds to noses.

He slackened pace by the Tineton tree,
(A vast hollow ash-tree grown in three),
He wriggled a shake and padded slow,
Not sure if the hounds were on or no.

A horn blew faint, then he heard the sounds
Of a cantering huntsman, lifting hounds,
The ploughman had raised his hat for sign,
And the hounds were lifted and on his line.
He heard the splash in the Pantry Brook,
And a man's voice: 'Thiccy's the line he took,'
And a clear 'Yoi Doit' and a whimpering quaver,
Though the lurcher dogs had dulled the savour.

The fox went off while the hounds made halt,
And the horses breathed and the field found fault,
But the whimpering rose to a crying crash
By the hollow ruin of Tineton Ash.
Then again the kettle drum horse hooves beat,
And the green blades bent to the fox's feet
And the cry rose keen not far behind
Of the 'Blood, Blood, Blood' in the fox-hounds' mind.

The fox was strong, he was full of running,
He could run for an hour and then be cunning,
But the cry behind him made him chill,
They were nearer now and they meant to kill.
They meant to run him until his blood
Clogged on his heart as his brush with mud,
Till his back bent up and his tongue hung flagging,
And his belly and brush were filthed from dragging.
Till he crouched stone-still, dead-beat and dirty,
With nothing but teeth against the thirty.
And all the way to that blinding end
He would meet with men and have none his friend.
Men to holloa and men to run him,
With stones to stagger and yells to stun him,
Men to head him, with whips to beat him,
Teeth to mangle and mouths to eat him.
And all the way, that wild high crying,
To cold his blood with the thought of dying,
The horn and the cheer, and the drum-like thunder,
Of the horsehooves stamping the meadows under.

He upped his brush and went with a will
For the Sarsen Stones on Wan Dyke Hill.

As he ran the meadow by Tineton Church,
A christening party left the porch,
They stood stock still as he pounded by,
They wished him luck but they thought he'd die.
The toothless babe in his long white coat
Looked delicate meat, the fox took note;
But the sight of them grinning there, pointing finger,
Made him put on steam till he went a stinger.

Past Tineton Church over Tineton Waste,
With the lolloping ease of a fox's haste,
The fur on his chest blown dry with the air,
His brush still up and his cheek-teeth bare.
Over the Waste where the ganders grazed,
The long swift lilt of his loping lazed,
His ears cocked up as his blood ran higher,
He saw his point, and his eyes took fire.
The Wan Dyke Hill with its fir tree barren,
Its dark of gorse and its rabbit warren,
The Dyke on its heave like a tightened girth,
And holes in the Dyke where a fox might earth.
He had rabbited there long months before,
The earths were deep and his need was sore,
The way was new, but he took a bearing,
And rushed like a blown ship billow-sharing.

Off Tineton Common to Tineton Dean,
Where the wind-hid elders pushed with green;
Through the Dean's thin cover across the lane,
And up Midwinter to King of Spain.
Old Joe at digging his garden grounds,
Said, 'A fox, being hunted; where be hounds?
O lord, my back, to be young again,
'Stead a zellin zider in King of Spain.
O hark, I hear 'em, O sweet, O sweet.
Why there be redcoat in Gearge's wheat.
And there be redcoat, and there they gallop.
Thur go a browncoat down a wallop.
Quick, Ellen, Quick, Come Susan, fly.
Here'm hounds. I zeed the fox go by,
Go by like thunder, go by like blasting,

With his girt white teeth all looking ghasting.
Look there come hounds. Hark, hear 'em crying,
Lord, belly to stubble, ain't they flying.
There's huntsman, there. The fox come past,
(As I was digging) as fast as fast.
He's only been gone a minute by;
A girt dark dog as pert as pye.'

Ellen and Susan came out scattering
Brooms and dustpans till all was clattering;
They saw the pack come head to foot
Running like racers, nearly mute;
Robin and Dansey quartering near,
All going gallop like startled deer.
A half-dozen flitting scarlets shewing
In the thin green Dean where the pines were growing.
Black coats and brown coats thrusting and spurring,
Sending the partridge coveys whirring,
Then a rattle up hill and a clop up lane,
It emptied the bar of the King of Spain.

Tom left his cider, Dick left his bitter,
Granfer James left his pipe and spitter,
Out they came from the sawdust floor,
They said, 'They'm going.' They said, 'O Lor.'

The fox raced on, up the Barton Balks,
With a crackle of kex in the nettle stalks,
Over Hammond's grass to the dark green line
Of the larch-wood smelling of turpentine.
Scratch Steven Larches, black to the sky,
A sadness breathing with one long sigh,
Grey ghosts of trees under funeral plumes,
A mist of twig over soft brown glooms.
As he entered the wood he heard the smacks,
Chip-Jar, of the fir-pole feller's axe,
He swerved to the left to a broad green ride,
Where a boy made him rush for the further side.
He swerved to the left, to the Barton Road,
But there were the timberers come to load.
Two timber carts and a couple of carters
With straps round their knees instead of garters.
He swerved to the right, straight down the wood,
The carters watched him, the boy hallooed.

He leaped from the larch-wood into tillage,
The cobbler's garden of Barton village.

The cobbler bent at his wooden foot,
Beating sprigs in a broken boot;
He wore old glasses with thick horn rim,
He scowled at his work for his sight was dim.
His face was dingy, his lips were grey,
From primming sparrowbills day by day,
As he turned his boot he heard a noise
At his garden-end, and he thought, 'It's boys.'

He saw his cat nip up on the shed,
Where her back arched up till it touched her head,
He saw his rabbit race round and round
Its little black box three feet from ground.
His six hens cluckered and flucked to perch,
'That's boys,' said cobbler, 'so I'll go search.'
He reached his stick and blinked in his wrath,
When he saw a fox in his garden path.

The fox swerved left and scrambled out,
Knocking crinked green shells from the Brussels Sprout,
He scrambled out through the cobbler's paling,
And up Pill's orchard to Purton's Tailing,
Across the plough at the top of bent,
Through the heaped manure to kill his scent,
Over to Aldams, up to Cappells,
Past Nursery Lot with its whitewashed apples,
Past Colston's Broom, past Gaunts, past Sheres,
Past Foxwhelps Oasts with their hooded ears,
Past Monk's Ash Clerewell, past Beggars Oak,
Past the great elms blue with the Hinton smoke,
Along Long Hinton to Hinton Green,
Where the windwashed steeple stood serene
With its golden bird still sailing air,
Past Banner Barton, past Chipping Bare,
Past Maddings Hollow, down Dundry Dip,
And up Goose Grass to the Sailing Ship.

The three black firs of the Ship stood still
On the bare chalk heave of the Dundry Hill,
The fox looked back as he slackened past
The scaled red-bole of the mizen-mast.

There they were coming, mute but swift,
A scarlet smear in the blackthorn rift,
A white horse rising, a dark horse flying,
And the hungry hounds too tense for crying.
Stormcock leading, his stern spear-straight,
Racing as though for a piece of plate,
Little speck horsemen field on field;
Then Dansey viewed him and Robin squealed.

At the 'View Halloo' the hounds went frantic,
Back went Stormcock and up went Antic,
Up went Skylark as Antic sped
It was zest to blood how they carried head.
Skylark drooped as Maroon drew by,
Their hackles lifted, they scored to cry.

The fox knew well, that before they tore him,
They should try their speed on the downs before him,
There were three more miles to the Wan Dyke Hill,
But his heart was high, that he beat them still.
The wind of the downland charmed his bones
So off he went for the Sarsen Stones.

The moan of the three great firs in the wind,
And the 'Ai' of the fox-hounds died behind,
Wind-dapples followed the hill-wind's breath
On the Kill Down gorge where the Danes found death;
Larks scattered up; the peewits feeding
Rose in a flock from the Kill Down Steeding.
The hare leaped up from her form and swerved
Swift left for the Starveall, harebell-turved.
On the wind-bare thorn some longtails prinking
Cried sweet, as though windblown glass were chinking.
Behind came thudding and loud halloo
Or a cry from hounds as they came to view.

The pure clean air came sweet to his lungs,
Till he thought foul scorn of those crying tongues,
In a three mile more he would reach the haven
In the Wan Dyke croaked on by the raven,
In a three mile more he would make his berth
On the hard cool floor of a Wan Dyke earth,
Too deep for spade, too curved for terrier,
With the pride of the race to make rest the merrier.

In a three mile more he would reach his dream,
So his game heart gulped and he put on steam.

Like a rocket shot to a ship ashore,
The lean red bolt of his body tore,
Like a ripple of wind running swift on grass,
Like a shadow on wheat when a cloud blows past,
Like the turn at the buoy in a cutter sailing,
When the bright green gleam lips white at the railing,
Like the April snake whipping back to sheath,
Like the gannets' hurtle on fish beneath,
Like a kestrel chasing, like a sickle reaping,
Like all things swooping, like all things sweeping,
Like a hound for stay, like a stag for swift,
With his shadow beside like spinning drift.

Past the gibbet-stock all stuck with nails,
Where they hanged in chains what had hung at jails,
Past Ashmundshowe where Ashmund sleeps,
And none but the tumbling peewit weeps,
Past Curlew Calling, the gaunt grey corner
Where the curlew comes as a summer mourner,
Past Blowbury Beacon shaking his fleece,
Where all winds hurry and none brings peace,
Then down, on the mile-long green decline
Where the turf's like spring and the air's like wine,
Where the sweeping spurs of the downland spill
Into Wan Brook Valley and Wan Dyke Hill.

On he went with a galloping rally
Past Maesbury Clump for Wan Brook Valley,
The blood in his veins went romping high
'Get on, on, on to the earth or die.'
The air of the downs went purely past,
Till he felt the glory of going fast,
Till the terror of death, though there indeed,
Was lulled for a while by his pride of speed,
He was romping away from hounds and hunt,
He had Wan Dyke Hill and his earth in front,
In a one mile more when his point was made,
He would rest in safety from dog or spade,
Nose between paws he would hear the shout
Of the 'Gone to earth' to the hounds without,
The whine of the hounds, and their cat-feet gadding,

Scratching the earth, and their breath pad-padding,
He would hear the horn call hounds away,
And rest in peace till another day.

In one mile more he would lie at rest,
So for one mile more he would go his best.
He reached the dip at the long droop's end
And he took what speed he had still to spend.

So down past Maesbury beech-clump grey,
That would not be green till the end of May,
Past Arthur's Table, the white chalk boulder
Where pasque flowers purple the down's grey shoulder
Past Quichelm's Keeping, past Harry's Thorn
To Thirty Acre all thin with corn.

As he raced the corn towards Wan Dyke Brook,
The pack had view of the way he took,
Robin hallooed from the downland's crest,
He capped them on till they did their best.
The quarter-mile to the Wan Brook's brink
Was raced as quick as a man can think.

And here, as he ran to the huntsman's yelling,
The fox first felt that the pace was telling,
His body and lungs seemed all grown old,
His legs less certain, his heart less bold,
The hound-noise nearer, the hill slope steeper,
The thud in the blood of his body deeper,
His pride in his speed, his joy in the race
Were withered away, for what use was pace?
He had run his best, and the hounds ran better.
Then the going worsened, the earth was wetter.
Then his brush drooped down till it sometimes dragged
And his fur felt sick and his chest was tagged
With taggles of mud, and his pads seemed lead,
It was well for him he'd an earth ahead.

Down he went to the brook and over,
Out of the corn and into the clover,
Over the slope that the Wan Brook drains,
Past Battle Tump where they earthed the Danes,
Then up the hill that the Wan Dyke rings
Where the Sarsen Stones stand grand like kings.

Seven Sarsens of granite grim,
As he ran them by they looked at him;
As he leaped the lip of their earthen paling
The hounds were gaining and he was failing.

He passed the Sarsens, he left the spur,
He pressed uphill to the blasted fir,
He slipped as he leaped the hedge; he slithered…
'He's mine,' thought Robin, 'He's done; he's dithered.'

At the second attempt he cleared the fence,
He turned half-right where the gorse was dense,
He was leading hounds by a furlong clear.
He was past his best, but his earth was near.
He ran up gorse, to the spring of the ramp,
The steep green wall of the dead men's camp,
He sidled up it and scampered down
To the deep green ditch of the dead men's town.

Within, as he reached that soft green turf,
The wind, blowing lonely, moaned like surf,
Desolate ramparts rose up steep,
On either side, for the ghosts to keep.
He raced the trench, past the rabbit warren,
Close-grown with moss which the wind made barren,
He passed the spring where the rushes spread,
And there in the stones was his earth ahead.
One last short burst upon failing feet,
There life lay waiting, so sweet, so sweet,
Rest in a darkness, balm for aches.

The earth was stopped. It was barred with stakes.

With the hounds at head so close behind
He had to run as he changed his mind.
This earth, as he saw, was stopped, but still
There was one earth more on the Wan Dyke Hill.
A rabbit burrow a furlong on,
He could kennel there till the hounds were gone.
Though his death seemed near he did not blench
He upped his brush and he ran the trench.

He ran the trench while the wind moaned treble,
Earth trickled down, there were falls of pebble.
Down in the valley of that dark gash
The wind-withered grasses looked like ash.
Trickles of stones and earth fell down
In that dark alley of dead men's town.
A hawk arose from a fluff of feathers,
From a distant fold came a bleat of wethers.
He heard no noise from the hounds behind
But the hill-wind moaning like something blind.

He turned the bend in the hill, and there
Was his rabbit-hole with its mouth worn bare,
But there with a gun tucked under his arm
Was young Sid Kissop of Purlpits Farm,
With a white hob ferret to drive the rabbit
Into a net which was set to nab it.
And young Jack Cole peered over the wall
And loosed a pup with a 'Z'bite en, Saul,'
The terrier pup attacked with a will,
So the fox swerved right and away downhill.

Down from the ramp of the dyke he ran
To the brackeny patch where the gorse began,
Into the gorse, where the hill's heave hid
The line he took from the eyes of Sid;
He swerved downwind and ran like a hare
For the wind-blown spinney below him there.

He slipped from the gorse to the spinney dark
(There were curled grey growths on the oak tree bark)
He saw no more of the terrier pup.
But he heard men speak and the hounds come up.

He crossed the spinney with ears intent
For the cry of hounds on the way he went
His heart was thumping, the hounds were near now.
He could make no sprint at a cry and cheer now,
He was past his perfect, his strength was failing,
His brush sag-sagged and his legs were ailing.
He felt, as he skirted dead men's town,
That in one mile more they would have him down.

Through the withered oaks' wind-crouching tops
He saw men's scarlet above the copse,
He heard men's oaths, yet he felt hounds slacken
In the frondless stalks of the brittle bracken.
He felt that the unseen link which bound
His spine to the nose of the leading hound,
Was snapped, that the hounds no longer knew
Which way to follow nor what to do;
That the threat of the hounds' teeth left his neck,
They had ceased to run, they had come to check,
They were quartering wide on the Wan Hill's bent.

The terrier's chase had killed his scent.

He heard bits chink as the horses shifted,
He heard hounds cast, then he heard hounds lifted,
But there came no cry from a new attack;
His heart grew steady, his breath came back.

He left the spinney and ran its edge,
By the deep dry ditch of the blackthorn hedge,
Then out of the ditch and down the meadow,
Trotting at ease in the blackthorn shadow.
Over the track called Godsdown Road,
To the great grass heave of the gods' abode,
He was moving now upon land he knew
Up Clench Royal and Morton Tew
The Pol Brook, Cheddesdon, and East Stoke Church,
High Clench St. Lawrence and Tinker's Birch,
Land he had roved on night by night,
For hot blood suckage or furry bite,
The threat of the hounds behind was gone;
He breathed deep pleasure and trotted on.

While young Sid Kissop thrashed the pup,
Robin on Pip came heaving up,
And found his pack spread out at check.
'I'd like to wring your terrier's neck,'
He said, 'You see? He's spoiled our sport.
He's killed the scent.' He broke off short,
And stared at hounds and at the valley.
No jay or magpie gave a rally
Down in the copse, no circling rooks
Rose over fields; old Joyful's looks
Were doubtful in the gorse, the pack
Quested both up and down and back.
He watched each hound for each small sign.
They tried, but could not hit the line,
The scent was gone. The field took place
Out of the way of hounds. The pace
Had tailed them out; though four remained:–
Sir Peter, on White Rabbit stained
Red from the brooks, Bill Ridden cheery,
Hugh Colway with his mare dead weary,
The Colonel with Marauder beat.
They turned towards a thud of feet;
Dansey, and then young Cothill came,
(His chestnut mare was galloped tame).
'There's Copse, a field behind,' he said.
'Those last miles put them all to bed.
They're strung along the downs like flies.'
Copse and Nob Manor topped the rise.
'Thank God, a check,' they said, 'at last.'

'They cannot own it; you must cast,'
Sir Peter said. The soft horn blew,
Tom turned the hounds upwind; they drew
Upwind, downhill, by spinney side.
They tried the brambled ditch; they tried
The swamp, all choked with bright green grass
And clumps of rush and pools like glass,
Long since, the dead men's drinking pond.
They tried the White Leaved Oak beyond,
But no hound spoke to it or feathered.
The horse heads drooped like horses tethered,
The men mopped brows. 'An hour's hard run.
Ten miles,' they said, 'we must have done.

It's all of six from Colston's Gorses.'
The lucky got their second horses.

The time ticked by. 'He's lost,' they muttered.
A pheasant rose. A rabbit scuttered.
Men mopped their scarlet cheeks and drank.

They drew downwind along the bank,
(The Wan Way) on the hill's south spur,
Grown with dwarf oak and juniper
Like dwarves alive, but no hound spoke.
The seepings made the ground one soak.
They turned the spur; the hounds were beat.
Then Robin shifted in his seat
Watching for signs, but no signs shewed.
'I'll lift across the Godsdown Road,
Beyond the spinney,' Robin said.
Tom turned them; Robin went ahead.

Beyond the copse a great grass fallow
Stretched towards Stoke and Cheddesdon Mallow,
A rolling grass where hounds grew keen.
'Yoi doit, then; this is where he's been,'
Said Robin, eager at their joy.
'Yooi, Joyful, lad, Yoi, Cornerboy.
They're onto him.'
                           At his reminders
The keen hounds hurried to the finders.
The finding hounds began to hurry,
Men jammed their hats prepared to scurry,
The 'Ai Ai' of the cry began.
Its spirit passed to horse and man,
The skirting hounds romped to the cry.
Hound after hound cried 'Ai Ai Ai,'
Till all were crying, running, closing,
Their heads well up and no heads nosing,
Joyful ahead with spear-straight stern.
They raced the great slope to the burn
Robin beside them, Tom behind,
Pointing past Robin down the wind.

For there, two furlongs on, he viewed
On Holy Hill or Cheddesdon Rood
Just where the ploughland joined the grass,

A speck down the first furrow pass,
A speck the colour of the plough.
'Yonder he goes. We'll have him now,'
He cried. The speck passed slowly on,
It reached the ditch, paused, and was gone.

Then down the slope and up the Rood,
Went the hunt's gallop. Godsdown Wood
Dropped its last oak-leaves at the rally.
Over the Rood to High Clench Valley
The gallop led; the red-coats scattered,
The fragments of the hunt were tattered
Over five fields, ev'n since the check.
'A dead fox or a broken neck,'
Said Robin Dawe, 'Come up, the Dane.'
The hunter leant against the rein,
Cocking his ears, he loved to see
The hounds at cry. The hounds and he
The chiefs in all that feast of pace.

The speck in front began to race.

The fox heard hounds get onto his line,
And again the terror went down his spine,
Again the back of his neck felt cold,
From the sense of the hounds' teeth taking hold.
But his legs were rested, his heart was good,
He had breath to gallop to Mourne End Wood,
It was four miles more, but an earth at end,
So he put on pace down the Rood Hill Bend.

Down the great grass slope which the oak trees dot,
With a swerve to the right from the keeper's cot,
Over High Clench brook in its channel deep,
To the grass beyond, where he ran to sheep.

The sheep formed line like a troop of horse
They swerved, as he passed, to front his course
From behind, as he ran, a cry arose,
'See the sheep, there. Watch them. There he goes.'

He ran the sheep that their smell might check
The hounds from his scent and save his neck,
But in two fields more he was made aware
That the hounds still ran; Tom had viewed him there.

Tom had held them on through the taint of sheep,
They had kept his line, as they meant to keep,
They were running hard with a burning scent,
And Robin could see which way he went.
The pace that he went brought strain to breath,
He knew as he ran that the grass was death.

He ran the slope towards Morton Tew
That the heave of the hill might stop the view,
Then he doubled down to the Blood Brook red,
And swerved upstream in the brook's deep bed.
He splashed the shallows, he swam the deeps,
He crept by banks as a moorhen creeps,
He heard the hounds shoot over his line,
And go on, on, on, towards Cheddesdon Zine.

In the minute's peace he could slacken speed,
The ease from the strain was sweet indeed.
Cool to the pads the water flowed,
He reached the bridge on the Cheddesdon Road.

As he came to light from the culvert dim,
Two boys on the bridge looked down on him;
They were young Bill Ripple and Harry Meun,
'Look, there be squirrel, a-swimmin', see un.'
'Noa, ben't a squirrel, be fox, be fox.
Now, Hal, get pebble, we'll give en socks.'
'Get pebble, Billy, dub un a plaster;
There's for thy belly, I'll learn 'ee, master.'

The stones splashed spray in the fox's eyes,
He raced from brook in a burst of shies,
He ran for the reeds in the withy car,
Where the dead flags shake and the wild-duck are.

He pushed through the reeds which cracked at his passing,
To the High Clench Water, a grey pool glassing,
He heard Bill Ripple in Cheddesdon Road,
Shout, 'This way, huntsmen, it's here he goed.'

Then 'Leu Leu Leu' went the soft horn's laughter,
The hounds (they had checked) came romping after,
The clop of the hooves on the road was plain,
Then the crackle of reeds, then cries again.

A whimpering first, then Robin's cheer,
Then the 'Ai Ai Ai;' they were all too near;
His swerve had brought but a minute's rest
Now he ran again, and he ran his best.

With a crackle of dead dry stalks of reed
The hounds came romping at topmost speed
The redcoats ducked as the great hooves skittered
The Blood Brook's shallows to sheets that glittered;
With a cracking whip and a 'Hoik, Hoik, Hoik,
Forrard,' Tom galloped. Bob shouted, 'Yoick.'
Like a running fire the dead reeds crackled
The hounds' heads lifted, their necks were hackled.
Tom cried to Bob as they thundered through,
'He is running short, we shall kill at Tew.'
Bob cried to Tom as they rode in team,
'I was sure, that time, that he turned upstream.
As the hounds went over the brook in stride
I saw old Daffodil fling to side
So I guessed at once, when they checked beyond.'

The ducks flew up from the Morton Pond.
The fox looked up at their tailing strings,
He wished (perhaps) that a fox had wings.
Wings with his friends in a great V straining
The autumn sky when the moon is gaining;
For better the grey sky's solitude,
Than to be two miles from the Mourne End Wood
With the hounds behind, clean-trained to run,
And your strength half spent and your breath half done.
Better the reeds and the sky and water
Than that hopeless pad from a certain slaughter,
At the Morton Pond the fields began,
Long Tew's green meadows; he ran; he ran.

First the six green fields that make a mile,
With the lip-full Clench at the side the while,
With rooks above, slow-circling, shewing
The world of men where a fox was going;
The fields all empty, dead grass, bare hedges,
And the brook's bright gleam in the dark of sedges.
To all things else he was dumb and blind,
He ran, with the hounds a field behind.

At the sixth green field came the long slow climb,
To the Mourne End Wood, as old as time;
Yew woods dark, where they cut for bows,
Oak woods green with the mistletoes,
Dark woods evil, but burrowed deep
With a brock's earth strong, where a fox might sleep.
He saw his point on the heaving hill,
He had failing flesh and a reeling will,
He felt the heave of the hill grow stiff,
He saw black woods, which would shelter – if –
Nothing else, but the steepening slope,
And a black line nodding, a line of hope
The line of the yews on the long slope's brow,
A mile, three-quarters, a half-mile now.

A quarter-mile, but the hounds had viewed.
They yelled to have him this side the wood.
Robin capped them, Tom Dansey steered them
With a 'Yooi, Yooi, Yooi,' Bill Ridden cheered them.
Then up went hackles as Shatterer led,
'Mob him,' cried Ridden, 'the wood's ahead.

Turn him, damn it; Yooi, beauties, beat him
O God, let them get him; let them eat him
O God,' cried Ridden, 'I'll eat him stewed,
If you'll let us get him this side the wood.'

But the pace, uphill, made a horse like stone,
The pack went wild up the hill alone.

Three hundred yards, and the worst was past,
The slope was gentler and shorter-grassed,
The fox saw the bulk of the woods grow tall
On the brae ahead, like a barrier-wall.
He saw the skeleton trees show sky,
And the yew trees darken to see him die
And the line of the woods go reeling black
There was hope in the woods, and behind, the pack.

Two hundred yards, and the trees grew taller,
Blacker, blinder, as hope grew smaller,
Cry seemed nearer, the teeth seemed gripping
Pulling him back, his pads seemed slipping.
He was all one ache, one gasp, one thirsting,
Heart on his chest-bones, beating, bursting;
The hounds were gaining like spotted pards
And the wood-hedge still was a hundred yards.

The wood-hedge black was a two-year, quick
Cut-and-laid that had sprouted thick
Thorns all over, and strongly plied,
With a clean red ditch on the take-off side.

He saw it now as a redness, topped
With a wattle of thorn-work spiky cropped,
Spiky to leap on, stiff to force,
No safe jump for a failing horse,
But beyond it, darkness of yews together,
Dark green plumes over soft brown feather,
Darkness of woods where scents were blowing
Strange scents, hot scents, of wild things going,
Scents that might draw these hounds away.
So he ran, ran, ran to that clean red clay.

Still, as he ran, his pads slipped back,
All his strength seemed to draw the pack,

The trees drew over him dark like Norns,
He was over the ditch and at the thorns.

He thrust at the thorns, which would not yield,
He leaped, but fell, in sight of the field,
The hounds went wild as they saw him fall,
The fence stood stiff like a Bucks flint wall.

He gathered himself for a new attempt,
His life before was an old dream dreamt,
All that he was was a blown fox quaking,
Jumping at thorns too stiff for breaking,
While over the grass in crowd, in cry,
Came the grip teeth grinning to make him die,
The eyes intense, dull, smouldering red,
The fell like a ruff round each keen head,
The pace like fire, and scarlet men
Galloping, yelling, 'Yooi, eat him, then.'

He gathered himself, he leaped, he reached
The top of the hedge like a fish-boat beached.
He steadied a second and then leaped down
To the dark of the wood where bright things drown.

He swerved, sharp right, under young green firs.
Robin called on the Dane with spurs,
He cried, 'Come, Dansey; if God's not good,
We shall change our fox in this Mourne End Wood.'
Tom cried back as he charged like spate,
'Mine can't jump that, I must ride to gate.'
Robin answered, 'I'm going at him.
I'll kill that fox, if it kills me, drat him.
We'll kill in covert. Gerr on, now, Dane.'
He gripped him tight and he made it plain,
He slowed him down till he almost stood
While his hounds went crash into Mourne End Wood.

Like a dainty dancer with footing nice,
The Dane turned side for a leap in twice.
He cleared the ditch to the red clay bank,
He rose at the fence as his quarters sank,
He barged the fence as the bank gave way
And down he came in a fall of clay.

Robin jumped off him and gasped for breath;
He said, 'That's lost him as sure as death.
They've over-run him. Come up, the Dane.
We'll kill him yet, if we ride to Spain.'

He scrambled up to his horse's back,
He thrust through cover, he called his pack,
He cheered them on till they made it good,
Where the fox had swerved inside the wood.

The fox knew well as he ran the dark,
That the headlong hounds were past their mark;
They had missed his swerve and had over-run.
But their devilish play was not yet done.

For a minute he ran and heard no sound,
Then a whimper came from a questing hound,
Then a 'This way, beauties,' and then 'Leu Leu,'
The floating laugh of the horn that blew.
Then the cry again and the crash and rattle
Of the shrubs burst back as they ran to battle.
Till the wood behind seemed risen from root,
Crying and crashing to give pursuit,
Till the trees seemed hounds and the air seemed cry,
And the earth so far that he needs must die,
Die where he reeled in the woodland dim
With a hound's white grips in the spine of him.
For one more burst he could spurt, and then
Wait for the teeth, and the wrench, and men.

He made his spurt for the Mourne End rocks,
The air blew rank with the taint of fox;
The yews gave way to a greener space
Of great stones strewn in a grassy place.
And there was his earth at the great grey shoulder,
Sunk in the ground, of a granite boulder.
A dry deep burrow with rocky roof,
Proof against crowbars, terrier-proof,
Life to the dying, rest for bones.

The earth was stopped; it was filled with stones.

Then, for a moment, his courage failed,
His eyes looked up as his body quailed,

Then the coming of death, which all things dread,
Made him run for the wood ahead.

The taint of fox was rank on the air,
He knew, as he ran, there were foxes there.
His strength was broken, his heart was bursting,
His bones were rotten, his throat was thirsting,
His feet were reeling, his brush was thick
From dragging the mud, and his brain was sick.

He thought as he ran of his old delight
In the wood in the moon in an April night,
His happy hunting, his winter loving,
The smells of things in the midnight roving,
The look of his dainty-nosing, red
Clean-felled dam with her footpad's tread,
Of his sire, so swift, so game, so cunning,
With craft in his brain and power of running,
Their fights of old when his teeth drew blood.
Now he was sick, with his coat all mud.

He crossed the covert, he crawled the bank,
To a meuse in the thorns and there he sank,
With his ears flexed back and his teeth shown white,
In a rat's resolve for a dying bite.

And there, as he lay, he saw the vale,
That a struggling sunlight silvered pale,
The Deerlip Brook like a strip of steel,
The Nun's Wood Yews where the rabbits squeal,
The great grass square of the Roman Fort,
And the smoke in the elms at Crendon Court.

And above the smoke in the elm-tree tops,
Was the beech-clump's blur, Blown Hilcote Copse,
Where he and his mates had long made merry
In the bloody joys of the rabbit-herry.

And there as he lay and looked, the cry
Of the hounds at head came rousing by;
He bent his bones in the blackthorn dim –

But the cry of the hounds was not for him.
Over the fence with a crash they went,

Belly to grass, with a burning scent,
Then came Dansey, yelling to Bob,
'They've changed, O damn it, now here's a job.'
And Bob yelled back, 'Well, we cannot turn 'em,
It's Jumper and Antic, Tom; we'll learn 'em.
We must just go on, and I hope we kill.'
They followed hounds down the Mourne End Hill.

The fox lay still in the rabbit-meuse,
On the dry brown dust of the plumes of yews.
In the bottom below a brook went by,
Blue, in a patch, like a streak of sky.
There, one by one, with a clink of stone
Came a red or dark coat on a horse half blown.
And man to man with a gasp for breath
Said, 'Lord, what a run. I'm fagged to death.'

After an hour, no riders came,
The day drew by like an ending game;
A robin sang from a pufft red breast,
The fox lay quiet and took his rest.
A wren on a tree-stump carolled clear,
Then the starlings wheeled in a sudden sheer,
The rooks came home to the twiggy hive
In the elm-tree tops which the winds do drive.
Then the noise of the rooks fell slowly still,
And the lights came out in the Clench Brook Mill;
Then a pheasant cocked, then an owl began
With the cry that curdles the blood of man.

The stars grew bright as the yews grew black,
The fox rose stiffly and stretched his back.
He flaired the air, then he padded out
To the valley below him dark as doubt,
Winter-thin with the young green crops,
For Old Cold Crendon and Hilcote Copse.

As he crossed the meadows at Naunton Larking,
The dogs in the town all started barking,
For with feet all bloody and flanks all foam,
The hounds and the hunt were limping home;
Limping home in the dark, dead-beaten,
The hounds all rank from a fox they'd eaten,
Dansey saying to Robin Dawe,

'The fastest and longest I ever saw.'
And Robin answered, 'O Tom, 't was good,
I thought they'd changed in the Mourne End Wood,
But now I feel that they did not change.
We've had a run that was great and strange;
And to kill in the end, at dusk, on grass.
We'll turn to The Cock and take a glass,
For the hounds, poor souls, are past their forces.
And a gallon of ale for our poor horses,
And some bits of bread for the hounds, poor things,
After all they've done (for they've done like kings),
Would keep them going till we get in.
We had it alone from Nun's Wood Whin.'
Then Tom replied, 'If they changed or not,
There've been few runs longer and none more hot,
We shall talk of today until we die.'

The stars grew bright in the winter sky,
The wind came keen with a tang of frost,
The brook was troubled for new things lost,
The copse was happy for old things found,
The fox came home and he went to ground.

And the hunt came home and the hounds were fed,
They climbed to their bench and went to bed,
The horses in stable loved their straw.
'Good-night, my beauties,' said Robin Dawe.

Then the moon came quiet and flooded full
Light and beauty on clouds like wool,
On a feasted fox at rest from hunting,
In the beech wood grey where the brocks were grunting.

The beech wood grey rose dim in the night
With moonlight fallen in pools of light,
The long-dead leaves on the ground were rimed.
A clock struck twelve and the church-bells chimed.

Letter to A.H. Higginson, 1920

Boars Hill, Oxford, England.
January 13th, 1920

Dear Mr. Higginson

Through the kindness of friends, I have seen your very generous praise of my poem, *Reynard the Fox*. I thank you for the kind things you say, and for your spirited and chivalrous defense.

Since you express a hope that I will write to you, to tell you whether I hunt, I send you this letter.

I have never ridden since I was a boy, and was then never allowed to ride to hounds. My father hunted, and drew delightful sketches of hunting. I was for seven years close to a Kennels, and saw hounds every day. For a second term of seven years, though not quite so close to the Kennels, I was within a mile of them. I followed the hounds on foot whenever I could. I have taken a footman's modest part in countless hunts, and have also hunted on a bicycle. When one knows, as I did, every inch of the wide country-side, every path, stile, gate and gap, as well as the workings of a fox's mind, one can hunt, even on foot, with great success, on cold-hunting days. One has a chance in all rather slow four to six mile points, and then, even in quite good things, luck sometimes comes to one. The fox might be headed, or changed, or go to ground, or the scent might fail and slow things down for one.

After all, poetry is not a written record of what one does. Were it so, Shakespeare would have been hanged for murder and Sophocles for incest. Poetry is the spiritual enjoyment of what one understands. I wrote my tale of the Fox because I felt deeply the beauty and the life of hunting.

I was very deeply pleased by your letter. Thank you for it.

Yours sincerely

John Masefield

Source: *ed.* Higginson, A.H. *As Hounds Ran*, New York: Huntington Press, 1930, pp. [225]–226.

Fox-Hunting, 1920

I have been asked to write why I wrote this poem of *Reynard the Fox*. As a man grows older, life becomes more interesting but less easy to know; for, late in life, even the strongest yields to the habit of his compartment. When he cannot range through all society, from the court to the gutter, a man must go where all society meets, as at the Pilgrimage, the Festival or the Game. Here in England the Game is both a festival and an occasion of pilgrimage. A man wanting to set down a picture of the society of England will find his models at the games.

What are the English games? The man's game is Association football; the woman's game, perhaps, hockey or lacrosse. Golf I regard more as a symptom of a happy marriage than a game. Cricket, which was once widely popular among both sexes has lost its hold, except among the young. The worst of all these games is that few can play them at a time.

But in the English country, during the autumn, winter and early spring of each year, the main sport is fox-hunting, which is not like cricket or football, a game for a few and a spectacle for many, but something in which all who come may take a part, whether rich or poor, mounted or on foot. It is a sport loved and followed by both sexes, all ages and all classes. At a fox-hunt, and nowhere else in England, except perhaps at a funeral, can you see the whole of the land's society brought together, focussed for the observer, as the Canterbury pilgrims were for Chaucer.

This fact made the subject attractive. The fox-hunt gave an opportunity for a picture or pictures of the members of an English community.

Then to all Englishmen who have lived in a hunting country, hunting is in the blood, and the mind is full of it. It is the most beautiful and the most stirring sight to be seen in England. In the ports, as at Falmouth, there are ships under sail, under way, coming or going, beautiful unspeakably. In the country, especially on the great fields on the lower slopes of the Downland, the teams of the ploughmen may be seen bowing forward on a skyline, and this sight can never fail to move one by its majesty of beauty. But in neither of these sights of beauty is there the bright colour and swift excitement of the hunt, nor the thrill of the horn, and the cry of the hounds ringing into the elements of the soul. Something in the hunt wakens memories hidden in the marrow, racial memories, of when one hunted for the tribe, animal memories, perhaps, of when one hunted with the pack, or was hunted.

Hunting has always been popular here in England. In ancient times it was necessary. Wolves, wild boar, foxes and deer had to be kept down. To hunt was then the social duty of the mounted man, when he was not engaged in war. It was also the opportunity of all other members of the community to have a good time in the open, with a feast or a new fur at the end, to crown the pleasure.

Since arms of precision were made, hunting on horseback with hounds has perhaps been unnecessary everywhere, but it is not easy to end a pleasure rooted in the instincts of men. Hunting has continued, and probably will continue, in this country and in Ireland. It is rapidly becoming a national sport in the United States.

Some have written, that hunting is the sport of the wealthy man. Some wealthy men hunt, no doubt, but they are not the backbone of the sport, so much as those who love and use horses. Parts of this country, of Ireland and of the United States are more than ordinarily good pasture, fitted for the breeding of horses, beyond most other places in the world. Hardly anywhere else is the climate so equable, the soil so right for the feet of colts and the grass so good. Where these conditions exist, men will breed horses and use them. Men who breed good horses will ride, jump and test them, and will invent means of riding, jumping and testing them, the steeplechase, the circus, the contests at fairs and shows, the point-to-point meeting, and they will preserve, if possible, any otherwise dying sport which offers such means.

I have mentioned several reasons why fox-hunting should be popular: (a) that it is a social business, at which the whole community may and does attend in vast numbers in a pleasant mood of goodwill, good humour and equality, and during which all may go anywhere, into ground otherwise shut to them; (b) that it is done in the winter, at a season when other social gatherings are difficult, and in country districts where no buildings, except the churches, could contain the numbers assembled; (c) that it is most beautiful to watch, so beautiful that perhaps very few of the acts of men can be so lovely to watch nor so exhilarating. The only thing to be compared with it, in this country, is the sword dance, the old heroical dancing of the young men, still practised, in all its splendour of wild beauty, in some country places; (d) that we are a horse-loving people who have loved horses as we have loved the sea, and have made, in the course of generations, a breed of horse, second to none in the world, for beauty and speed.

But besides all these reasons, there is another that brings many out hunting. This is the delight in hunting, in the working of hounds, by themselves or with the huntsman, to find and kill their fox. Though many men and women hunt in order to ride, many still ride in order to hunt.

Perhaps this delight in hunting was more general in the mid-eighteenth century, when hounds were much slower than at present. Then, the hunt was indeed a test of hounds and huntsman. The fox was not run down but hunted down. The great run then was that in which hounds and huntsman kept to their fox. The great run now is perhaps that in which some few riders keep with the hounds.

The ideal run of 1750 might have been described thus:–

Being in the current of Writing, I cannot but acquaint your Lorp of ye great Hunt there was, this Tuesday last there was a Week. Sure so great a day has not been seen here since The Day your Lorp's Father broke his Collar Bone at ye Park Wall. As Milton says:–

Well have we speeded, and o'er Hill and Dale
Forest and Field and Flood...
As far as Indus east, Euphrates west.

We had but dismle Weather of it, and so cold, as made Sir Harry observe, that it was an ill wind blew no-one any good. We met at ye Tailings. I had out my brown Horse. There was present Sir Anthony Smoaker; Mr. Jarvis of Copse Stile; William Travis; John Hawbuck; your Lorp's Friend, Dick Fancowe, and two of ye Red Coats from ye Barracks. Ye fair Sex was dismayed, it was said, by ye rudeness of ye Elements; they did not venture it.

On coming to draw Tailings Wood, Glider spoke to it, and Tom viewed him away for the Valley, being the old Dog Fox, with the white Mask, that beat us at Fubb's Field, the day your Lorp road Bluebell.

Now spoke the chearful Horn; and tuneful Hounds
Echoed, and Red Coats gallopped; stirring Scean,
Rude Health and Manly Wit together strive.

We went with the extream of Violence from Tailings Wood to ye small Coppice at Nap Hill where a Fellow put him from his Point, which gave Occasion to Sir Anthony to correct him. Ye little magpie Hound made it out in ye bog at ye back of ye Coppice, when again Hounds went at head through Long Stone Pastures as far as Tainton. Here we was delayed in ye Dear Park, the effluvia of ye Dear being extream strong and doubtless puzzling to the Noses of ye Hounds. And here I cannot but remark the skill with which ye Hounds worked it out till they had hit it off, a sight, as Mr. Jarvis remarked to me, worthy of the Admiration of an antient Philosopher, and of the eloquence of a most elegant Wit, or Poet. Leaving ye Dear Park, He made for Norton Cross, which he left on his left Hand, as though deciding for ye Hill. Crossing ye Hill, in Spite of ye Sheep, he was a little staggered by his being run by one of ye Shepherd's Doggs, a part of Creation that should not be tolerated, except in ye vision of ye Poet, as in a Pastoral or so. Here Joe Phillips, our Huntsman, made unavailing Casts, but by lifting to the Vineyard recovered him, when Hounds run him to Cow's Crookham, on your Lorp's Aston Estate.

By this Time your Lorp will understand our Distress. Dick Fancowe was in ye Brook at Norton, Mr. Jarvis' grey Horse had cast a Shoe, and one of ye Red Coats had broak his Liver in falling at a Fence. For a time we went about to recover him:–

> Now with attentive Nose the restless Hound
> Endeavours on the Scent, now here, now there,
> Scorning adulterat scents of lesser Prey.
> Now gloomy care invades the Huntsman's Face;
> And Sportsmen (jovial erst) on weary steeds
> Sit pensive.

Here might well be seen the Advantages of a judicious Breeding in Hounds, that neglects not the intellectual Part, but aims rather at a complete Animal than alone at Sinews and Corporeal Structure. That Blood of the Old Berkshire Glorious, which your Lorp's Father was wont to observe, was what he most stood by, next to our Constitution and the Protestant Succession, here stood us in good stead, for it was to Glorious ye Ninth, as well as to Growler and Glider (all of ye same royal strain) that we was indebted to ye happy Conclusion. They pushed him out of ye Stubbings at Cow's Crookham, where it seems he had taken Refuge in the Hollow of a decayed Tree. We chac't him thence upon ye Grass to Shepherd's Hey. Here he began to run short, being not a little apprehensive, lest his Foes should triumph, and snatch from him that Life, which he had so long nefariously pampered.

> On courtly Cock with all his household Train
> Of Hens obsequious, by the Hen Wife mourned.

The Sun, coming out from among ye Clouds, where he had been

too long hid, made (as was elegantly pretended by Sir Anthony), a Brightness, animating indeed to us, who carried the Sword of Justice, but, to the Criminal of our Pursuit, infinitely distressing. Then had your Lorp seen the gay Ardor of the Pack, as they came to the View, which they did about Stonepits, your Lorp would have said with the late elegant Poet:–

> Now o'er the glittering grass the sinewy Hound
> Shakes from his Feet the Dew and makes ye Woods resound.

To be brief, we killed in the Back Yard of ye Rummer and Glass after two and three quarters Hours of a Hunt such as (all are agreed) is not lightly to be parallelled. There was present at ye Death, beside Joe Phillips and Tom, Sir A. Smoaker, Mr. Wm. Travis and myself, all so extream distresst, Men and Beasts, that it was observed, it was a Marvel ye Horses were not dead. Such an Hunt, it was agreed, should be celebrated by an annual Dinner, at which the Toast of ye Chase might be rendered more than ordinary. Ye Hunt was upwards of Fifteen Miles in Length, and hath been the Subject of a Song, by a Member of Ye Hunt, which, as it would take long to transcribe, I forbear, hoping that we may sing it to your Lorp before (as ye Poet says):–

> Ye Vixen hath laid up her Cubs
> In snuggest Cave secure, when balmy Spring
> Wakens ye Meadows.

But to pass now from Celestial Pleasures to Worldly Cares, I have to acquaint your Lorp that your Lorp's Sister's Son, Mr. Parracombe, hath been killed by a Fall from his Horse, after Dinner with some Gentlemen, his particular Friends, an Affliction indeed great, humanly regarded, were it not also considered, how much happier his Lot must be, than in this Vale of Tears, etc. Ye Young Hounds thrive apace, and 't is thought the forward Season will be very favourable for their future Prey. I am, your Lorp's most obedient, Charles Cothill.

Perhaps the ideal run of the present time would be described as follows:–

A large field attended the Templecombe on Tuesday last at the popular meet at Heydigates. Will Mynors, late of the Parratts, carried the horn, in place of Tom Carling, now with Mr. Fletchers. A little time was spent in running through the shrubberies in the garden at Heydigates and then the word was given for the Cantlows. Will had no sooner put hounds into this famous cover than the dog pack proclaimed the joyous news. The fox, a traveller, was at once viewed away for the Three Oaks, across the rather heavy going of the pasture land. Coming to the Knock Brook, he swam it near Parson's Pleasure, going at a pace that let the knowing ones know that they were in for something out of the common. Keeping Snib's Farm on his right, he ran dead straight for Gallow's Wood, where some woodmen with their teams disturbed him. Swinging to his left, he went up the hill, through Bloody Lane, as though towards Dinsmore, but was again deflected by woodmen. Turning down the hill, he ran for the valley, passing Enderton Schoolhouse, the scholars of which were much cheered by the near prospect of the hunt. It was now evident that he was going for the Downs. Some of the less daring began to express the hope that he might be headed.

Scent from the first was burning and the pace a cracker. After leaving Enderton he made straight for the Danesway, past Snub's Titch and the Curlews, the green meadows of the pasture being sprinkled for miles with the relics of the field. He crossed the Roman Road at Orm's Oak and at once entered the Danesway, going at a pace which all thought could not last.

At the summit of the Danesway, known as the Gallows Point, hounds were brought to their noses, owing to the crossing of the line by sheep. A man working nearby was able to give the line and Will, lifting beyond the Lynchets, at once hit him off, and the hounds resumed their rush. From this point, they went almost exactly straight from the head of the Danesway to the fir copse by Arthur's Table. All this part of the run being across a rolling grass land, was at top speed, such as no horse could live with. At Arthur's Table, he was put from his earth by shooters who were netting the warren. As he could not get through them nor across the highway, then busy with traffic, He doubled down across the Starvings, where Will, the only man up at this point, although now three hundred yards behind hounds, caught sight of him on the opposite slope, romping away from hounds as though he would never grow old. On coming to the level, past Spinney's End, some of those who had been left at the Lynchets were able to rejoin, but were soon again cast out by the extreme violence of the going, which continued back across the Downs on a line obliquely parallel with his former track though a mile further to the south. It was supposed that he was going for the main earth in Bloody Acre Copse. Some workers in the strip at the edge of the copse headed him from this point. He swung left-handed past Staves acre, and so down to the valley by the shelving ground near Monk's Charwell. Here, for some unaccountable reason, the scent, which had been breast high, became catchy, and hounds lost their fox in the Osier cars at Charwell Springs. Later in the afternoon, while jogging home, a second fox was chopped in Mr. Parsloe's cover at Prince's Charwell. Hounds then went home.

The run from the Cantlows was not remarkable for any quality of hunting, but extremely so for pace and length. The distance run, from Cantlows Wood to the Osiers cannot have been less than thirteen miles, most of it indeed on the best going in the world, but at a racing pace, with nothing that can be called a check, the whole way. Some wished that the hounds might have been rewarded and others that Will Mynors might have crowned his opening gallop with a kill, but the general feeling was one of satisfaction that so game a fox escaped.

My own interest in fox-hunting began at a very early age. I was born in a good hunting country, partly woodland, partly pasture. My home, during my first seven years, was within half a mile of the kennels. I saw hounds on most days of my life. Hounds and hunting filled my imagination. I saw many meets, each as romantic as a circus. The huntsman and whipper-in seemed, then, to be the greatest men in the world, and those mild slaves, the hounds, the loveliest animals.

Often, as a little child, I saw and heard hounds hunting in and near a covert within sight of my old home. Once, when I was, perhaps, five years old, the fox was hunted into our garden, and those glorious beings in scarlet, as well as the hounds, were all about my lairs, like visitants from Paradise. The fox, on this occasion, went through a woodshed and escaped.

Later in my childhood, though I lived less near to the kennels, I was still within a mile of them, and saw hounds frequently at all seasons. In that hunting country, hunting was one of the interests of life; everybody knew about it, loved, followed, watched and discussed it. I went to many meets, and followed many hunts on foot. Each of these occasions is now distinct in my mind, with the colour and intensity of beauty. I saw many foxes starting off upon their runs, with the hounds close behind them. It was then that I learned to admire the ease and beauty of the speed of the fresh fox. That leisurely hurry, which romps away from the hardest-trained and swiftest fox-hounds without a visible effort, as though the hounds were weighted with lead, is the most lovely motion I have seen in an animal.

No fox was the original of my Reynard, but as I was much in the woods as a boy I saw foxes fairly often, considering that they are night-moving animals. Their grace, beauty, cleverness, and secrecy always thrilled me. Then that kind of grin which the mask wears made me credit them with an almost human humour. I thought the fox a merry devil, though a bloody one. Then he is one against many, who keeps his end up, and lives, often snugly, in spite of the world. The pirate and the nightrider are nothing to the fox, for romance and danger. This way of life of his makes it difficult to observe him in a free state at close quarters.

Once in the early spring in the very early morning, I saw a vixen playing with her cubs in the open space below a beech tree. Once I came upon a big dog-fox in a wheel-wright's yard, and watched him from within a few paces for some minutes. Twice I have watched half-grown cubs stalking rabbits. Twice out hunting, the fox has broken cover within three yards of me. These are the only free foxes which I have seen at close quarters. Foxes are night-moving animals. To know them well one should have cat's eyes and foxes' habits. By the imagination alone can men know foxes.

When I was about halfway through my poem, I found a dead dog-fox in a field near Cumnor Hurst. He was a fine full-grown fox in perfect condition; he must have picked up poison, for he had not been hunted, nor shot. On the pads of this dead fox, I noticed for the first time, the length and strength of a fox's claws.

Some have asked, whether the Ghost Heath Run is founded on any recorded run of any real Hunt. It is not. It is an imaginary run, in a country made up of many different pieces of country, some of them real, some of them imaginary. These real and imaginary fields, woods and brooks are taken as they exist, from Berkshire, where the fox lives, from Herefordshire where he was found, from Trapalanda, Gloucestershire, Buckinghamshire, Herefordshire, Worcestershire and Berkshire, where he ran, from Trapalanda, where he nearly died, and from a wild and beautiful corner in Berkshire where he rests from his run.

Some have asked when the poem was written. It was written between January 1 and May 20, 1919.

Some have asked, whether hunting will soon be abolished. I cannot tell, but I think it unlikely. People do not willingly resign their pleasures; men who breed horses will want to gallop them across country; hunting is a pleasure, as well as an opportunity to gallop; it is also an instinct in man. Some have thought that if 'small holdings,' that is 'produce gardens,' intensively cultivated, of about an acre apiece, became common, so that the country became more rigidly enclosed than at present, hunting would be made almost impossible. The small holding is generally the property of the small farmer (like the French cultivateur) who fences permanently with wire and cannot take down the wire during the hunting season, as most English farmers do at present. Small holdings will probably increase in number near towns, but farmers seem agreed that they can never become the national system of farming. The big farm, that can treat the great tract with machines, seems likely to be the farm of the future.

Even if the small holdings system were to prevail, it would hardly prevail over the sporting instincts of the race. Beauty and delight are stronger than the will to work. I am pretty sure that a pack of hounds, coming feathery by, at the heels of a whip's horse, while the field takes station and the huntsman, drawing his horn, prepares to hunt, would shake the resolve of most small holders, digging in their lots with thrift, industry and self-control. And then, if the huntsman were to blow his horn, and the hounds to feather on it and give tongue, and find, and go away at head, I am pretty sure that most of the small holders of this race would follow them. It is in this race to hunt.

I will conclude with a portrait of old Baldy Hill, the earth-stopper, who in the darkness of the early morning gads about on a pony, to 'stop' or 'put to' all earths, in which a hard-pressed fox might hide. In the poem, he enters when the hunt is about to start, but he is an important figure in a hunting community, and deserves a portrait. He may come here, at the beginning, for Baldy Hill is at the beginning of all fox-hunts. He dates from the beginning of Man. I have seen many a Baldy Hill in my life; he never fails to give me the feeling that he is Primitive Man survived. Primitive Man lived like that, in the woods, in the darkness, outwitting the wild things, while the rain dripped, and the owl cried, and the ghost came out from the grave. Baldy Hill stole the last litter of the last she-wolf to cross them with the King's hounds. He was in at the death of the last wild-boar. Sometimes, in looking at him, I think that his ashen stake must have a flint head, with which, on moony nights, he still creeps out, to rouse, it may be, the mammoth in his secret valley, or a sabretooth tiger, still caved in the woods. Life may and does shoot out into exotic forms, which may and do flower and perish. Perhaps when all the other forms of English life are gone, the Baldy Hill form, the stock form, will abide, still striding, head bent, with an ashen stake, after some wild thing, that has meat, or fur, or is difficult or dangerous to tackle.

Old Baldy Hill, the game old cock,
Still wore knee-gaiters and a smock.
He bore a five foot ashen stick
All scarred and pilled from many a click

Beating in covert with his sons
To drive the pheasants to the guns.

His face was beaten by the weather
To wrinkled red like bellows leather
He had a cold clear hard blue eye.
His snares made many a rabbit die.
On moony nights he found it pleasant
To stare the woods for roosting pheasant
Up near the tree-trunk on the bough.

He never trod behind a plough.
He and his two sons got their food
From wild things in the field and wood,
By snares, by ferrets put in holes,
By ridding pasture-land of moles;
By keeping, beating, trapping, poaching
And spaniel and retriever-coaching.

He and his sons had special merits
In breeding and in handling ferrets
Full many a snaky hob and jill
Had bit the thumbs of Baldy Hill.
He had no beard, but long white hair.
He bent in gait. He used to wear
Flowers in his smock, gold-clocks and peasen;
And spindle-fruit in hunting season.

I hope that he may live to wear spindle-fruit for many seasons to
come. Hunting makes more people happy than anything I know.
When people are happy together, I am quite certain that they build
up something eternal, something both beautiful and divine, which
weakens the power of all evil things upon this life of men and
women.

Source: 'Introduction', *Reynard the Fox*, 'new illustrated edition' [second
American edition (first American illustrated edition)], New York:
Macmillan, 1920, pp. v–xx.

Fox-Hunting: Conclusion

I wrote these words two years ago. I pull them out today after seeing once more the beauty of a fox-hunt. It has been a mild winter day, with sun and a westerly wind after a night of rain. Going down into the valley, the fields showed distinct, the trees in line, the grass dead, the earth in colour, in plough, under the black of the hedges, and fields of roots green and bright, exquisite to see. Far away, the line of the downs stood out in a bold and angry blue under the smoke of the sky. The sun shone over all this. The missel-thrushes sang in the ash trees. Then waverings of starlings and finches came over the road to me, with little creakings and ejaculations.

Wondering what had driven the birds over, I stopped, and heard in the field beyond the smack of a whip and the rate of a huntsman's voice, 'Yah–Milkmaid,' and there was the hunt coming over the pasture to the spinney. They were coming through a field grown about with thorn and high gorse, the gorse in Christmas blossom, and both gorse and thorn wet and dark from the rain. As I first saw them, they were coming out of a darkness into the light. The huntsman wore new scarlet, a little flecked with mud from the going. He rode a most noble dark brown hunter, who picked his way like a prince, and chafed, and burned his heart out for a find. The whip and the field went off upwind to the spinney end, while the huntsman took his hounds into cover, and gave them a note on his horn that went into men's hearts like a flake of fire.

In less than a minute the hounds were through the little spinney and away over the plough to draw the woods beyond. The field loitered on behind them, in an Indian file, along the drain of the plough. The scarlet of the hunt gave a beauty the more to the fields, the earth, the roots, and the black lines of the thorns. The water in the drain flashed about the horses' feet like little wings of fire.

In a minute or two they had passed into and through the wood, and so on to the bigger covers. I saw the soft scarlet bob away out of sight, with horsemen in Indian file loitering after.

All along the road, for the next two miles, I saw watchers at hedges, or standing in carts and cars, trying to catch a glimpse of them. In one field of roots, a shoot, both guns and keepers, had left its sport and had climbed up a rise to see the greater sport. They stood there with their spaniels, staring. In one ploughed field three plough-teams were halted against the sky, like bronzes of patience, while the ploughmen stood in the hedges watching.

All these were kindled and cheered by the beauty and glory of the horses, the colour, life and manhood of the sport, and the sympathy that linked that world to friendship and fellowship. Religion moved thus once, so did poetry.

Source: 'Fox-Hunting', *The Windmill* (edited by L. Callender), London: Heinemann, 1923, pp. 91–92.

Fox-Hunting (Book Reviews), 1921

[An unsigned book review by Masefield of: *Extracts from the Diary of a Huntsman* by Thomas Smith (Arnold. 21s. net.); *The Life of a Fox-hound* by John Mills (Philip Allan. 12s. 6d. net.); and *The Sport of our Ancestors* edited by Lord Willoughby de Broke (Constable. 21s. net.)]

Fox-hunting is still the most stirring sight to be seen in the English countryside. It is still the most beautiful, the least tainted, and, in a way, the most popular of all our sports; it is of the soil and comes out of our country life; perhaps few wish it away. It has survived a century and a half of change. It has survived the swift hound, the railway, the breechloading gun, barbed wire, and the war. It is surviving the tarmac road, artificial manures, and the use of petrol. It has been the joy and the poetry of six generations of our lustiest. It is in our blood and part of us; it is as native as Bewick and Old Crome and beer.

The three volumes before us show what the sport has meant to us in the last hundred years. Of the three, the first is the work of a man who knew his subject thoroughly, from many years of lively experience. Thomas Smith did not care much for writing, but went at it manfully from the fulness of his mind and made this book, which is sensible, downright, manful, matter of fact. Sometimes his mass of knowledge gets in his way, and then he shoulders through it in a choleric manner and goes on. His style is forceful and honest, reminding one of Cobbett, if one could image a Cobbett without the anger and the eloquence. Sometimes he will flounder into a long sentence and go cold-hunting over its plough for half a page and change the fox of his subject on the way. Like all men writing from a full memory, he is able to illustrate his meaning out of his experience. He drives his points home by anecdotes of things seen and done in the hunting-field before his own eyes. He flourished at a time when the old style, of hunting, was giving way to the new style, of riding. He had little patience with the new way; for what he loved was hunting the fox, the working of hounds, and the breeding of hounds 'for nose and stoutness.' His book makes one feel that he had little joy in riding. He writes of the horse as though it were little more than a machine necessary to his sport. Plainly the heart of the matter in his eyes was the finding, hunting, and beating of the fox. He shows a knowledge of the fox not to be equalled. He seems to have learned all the fox's tricks and habits, and then to have brooded upon each until he found the reason for them. This makes many of his pages read like the musings of an old, good hunting hound. These glimpses of understanding are shot with colour, so that they make an uncouth poetry. Perhaps hunting does always bring the men of our race more into that state of joy in which thought becomes poetry than any other of their actions or delights. The book is illustrated with some beautiful coloured plates from J.F. Herring and others.

The Life of a Fox-Hound is an early example of what is now called a nature-story. It must have first appeared about the time of *Black Beauty* and *The Story of the Robins*, but is better than either of those works, because the hound is less given to piety than Black Beauty or the Robins and tends less to edification. Mr. Mills wrote with knowledge of hounds and hunting, and with a good deal of understanding of the hound-mind and the pack-mind. Most of his story consists of imagined conversations between a young hound and a leader of the pack, varied with lively descriptions of hunting. Towards the end of the book the old hound becomes 'cruel dull and prosy' on the subjects of kennel-lameness and the feeding of hounds; otherwise the book is pleasant. It is illustrated by some pen-and-ink drawings by John Leech.

The Sport of our Ancestors is a collection of passages of verse and prose 'setting forth the sport of fox-hunting as our ancestors knew it.' Lord Willoughby de Broke, the maker of the collection, adds a short introduction and a number of spirited and sympathetic commentaries on the writers whose work he displays. These writers are all men of great repute in the hunting-field – Beckford, 'Nimrod,' Major Whyte-Melville, Mr. Egerton Warburton, Mr. Bromley-Davenport, and Anthony Trollope. The passages chosen are all most spirited pieces of description, but good as they are they all give place to the Editor's own delightful description in his notes on Mr. Egerton Warburton. This account of a run is surely the most charming ever written. Of the other pieces, some, like 'Nimrod's' 'The Chace' and Beckford's 'A Fox Chase,' are very well known. Others, like the two by Major Whyte-Melville, have been latterly neglected, as out of fashion, though both are sterling work. Warburton's poem 'Tar Wood' is full of life and go, and well deserves to be brought again before the public. Altogether Lord Willoughby de Broke has made a delightful book. Mr. G.D. Armour adds to its charm by some coloured plates and pencil drawings.

Source: *The Times Literary Supplement*, 29 December 1921, p. 871.

Foreword to As Hounds Ran, *1930*

Someone was saying the other day that during the last hundred and fifty years there have never been fewer than twenty-five thousand foxhunters in this country, meaning, by foxhunters, those who ride to hounds not less than once a week. To many, perhaps, the estimate may seem small, hardly more than six hundred to a county. It may be roughly right. But the numbers of lovers of the sport, who have turn'd out to watch it or to follow it, who have car'd for it and work't for it in any year of that century and a half, must be past telling, for it has been and is the national sport, of interest all the year round, of absorbing passion for half the year, and being of the essence of country life, ever beautiful, moving and of the stuff of poetry.

Being the national sport, it has inspired, during those five generations, something like a national art unlike anything produced elsewhere; an art moving and gay, like the sport which it portrays, for the people and of the people, the delight and the solace of rich and poor alike. Few houses and cottages in any country district are without one or more gay hunting prints. In the course of a lifetime, the Englishman sometimes comes to think that he has seen all the hunting prints that exist; then he may enter a wayside house or inn, and there will be one or even a series hitherto unknown to him, with something lively about it in its movement, or in the redness of its riders' coats, to make him look closely at it and long to own it.

Though there are many books about foxhunting, they are less well known than the prints, for many who will look at a print will not willingly read a book, even about a foxhunt. Some of the books are now difficult to find, or have become somewhat old-fashioned, since hunting has changed, or have lost their interest save in a few lively pages. No doubt many readers will be glad to have this book of Mr. Higginson's, which brings together from a variety of books (not all well known, and some very rare) a number of passages about foxhunting, each interesting in its way. Mr. Higginson is one of those welcome sportsmen who make sport an occasion of friendliness among nations. He is perhaps the first American to hunt an English pack and to introduce to English readers what Americans have written about this most English pastime. It is a pleasure to me to wish his book all happy success among the hunters of both lands.

Oxford, England
August, 1930

Source: *ed.* Higginson, A.H. *As Hounds Ran,* New York: Huntington Press, 1930, pp. [vii]–viii.

Note, 1946

The tale of the hunting of a fox was written near Oxford in the early part of 1919. It is, in part, an attempt to understand the mind of a shy wild animal when sorely beset; and, in part, a symbol of the free soul of humanity, then just escaped from extinction by the thoughtless, the debased and the determined leagued against it for four years of war. As the same fox has been more cruelly beset of late years, perhaps some image of his escape may be grateful at the present time...

Source: *Reynard the Fox with Selected Sonnets and Lyrics*, London: William Heinemann, 1946, p. [v].

Transcript of A Fox's Day, 1960

In the first half of the book called *Reynard the Fox*, I describe the gathering of an English society to a meet of fox-hounds, the arrival of the hounds and huntsmen, and the moving off of the company to find and chase a fox. Later in that book I tell of the fox, of his running before the hounds and of what happened. From some parts of this second half of the book I make the story that I here speak: a tale or description of a fox's day from a midnight to a midnight. I omit almost all mention of the people following the hounds and many other matters. As to the places mentioned, they are a medley of memory and imagination. The fox sets out from Berkshire, sleeps in Herefordshire, is chased through parts of Herefordshire, Buckinghamshire and Berkshire back into Herefordshire, he passes an anxious moment in Ireland, returns to Herefordshire and thence in a more leisurely way to Berkshire. From this point I tell the story of a fox's day.

On old Cold Crendon's windy tops
Grows wintrily Blown Hilcote Copse,
Wind-bitten beech with badger barrows,
Where brocks eat wasp-grubs with their marrows,
And foxes lie on short-grassed turf,
Nose between paws, to hear the surf
Of wind in the beeches drowsily.
There was my fox bred lustily
Three years before, and there he berthed
Under the beech-roots snugly earthed,
With a roof of flint and a floor of chalk,
And ten bitten hens' heads each on its stalk,
Some rabbits' paws, some fur from scuts,
A badger's corpse and a smell of guts.
And there on the night before my tale
He trotted out for a point in the vale.

He saw, from the cover edge, the valley
Go trooping down with its droops of sally
To the brimming river's lipping bend

And a light in the inn at Water's End.
He heard the owl go hunting by
And the shriek of the mouse the owl made die,
And the purr of the owl as he tore the red
Strings from between his claws and fed;
The smack of joy of the horny lips
Marbled green with the blobby strips.
He saw the farms where the dogs were barking,
Cold Crendon Court and Copsecote Larking;
The fault with the spring as bright as gleed,
Green-slash-laced with water-weed.
A glare in the sky still marked the town,
Though all folk slept and the blinds were down,
The street lamps watched the empty square,
The night-cat sang his evil there.

The fox's nose tipped up and round
Since smell is a part of sight and sound.
Delicate smells were drifting by,
The sharp nose flaired them heedfully;
Partridges in the clover stubble,
Crouched in a ring for the stoat to nubble.
Rabbit bucks beginning to box;
A scratching place for the pheasant cocks;
A hare in the dead grass near the drain,
And another smell like the spring again.

A faint rank taint like April coming,
It cocked his ears and his blood went drumming,
For somewhere out by Ghost Heath Stubs
Was a roving vixen wanting cubs.
Over the valley, floating faint
On a warmth of windflow came the taint,
He cocked his nose and he upped his brush,
And he went up wind like an April thrush.

By the Roman Road to Braiches Ridge
Where the fallen willow makes a bridge,
Over short sweet grass and worn flint arrows
And the three dumb hows of Tencombe Barrows.
And away and away with a rolling scramble,
Through the sally and up the bramble,
With a nose for the smells the night wind carried,
And his red fell clean for being married,

For clicketting time and Ghost Heath Wood,
Had put the violet in his blood.

By Tencombe Regis and Slaughters Court,
Through the great grass square of Roman Fort,
By Nun's Wood Yews and the Hungry Hill,
And the Corpse Way Stones all standing still.
Then with eyes like sparks and his blood awoken
Over the grass to Water's Oaken,
And over the hedge and into ride
To the Ghost Heath Wood for his roving bride.

Before the dawn he had loved and fed
And found a kennel and gone to bed
On a shelf of grass in a thick of gorse
That would bleed a hound and blind a horse.
There he slept in the mild west weather
With his nose and brush well tuckt together,
He slept like a child, who sleeps yet hears
With the self who needs neither eyes nor ears.

He slept while the pheasant cock untucked
His head from his wing, flew down and kukked,
And the drove of the starlings whirred and wheeled
Out of the ash-trees into field.
While with great black flags that flogged and paddled
The rooks went out to the plough and straddled,
Straddled wide on the moist red cheese,
Of the furrows driven at Uppat's Leas.

Down in the village, men awoke,
The chimneys breathed with a faint blue smoke,
The fox slept on, though tweaks and twitches
Due to his dreams, ran down his flitches.

The cows were milked and the yards were sluict,
And the cocks and hens let out of roost,
Windows were opened, mats were beaten,
All men's breakfasts were cooked and eaten,
But out in the gorse on the grassy shelf,
The sleeping fox looked after himself.

Deep in his dream he heard the life
Of the woodland seek for food or wife,

The hop of a stoat, a buck that thumped,
The squeal of a rat as a weasel jumped,
Cows in a byre, and distant men,
And Condicote church-clock striking ten.

At eleven o'clock a boy went past,
With a rough-haired terrier following fast
The boy's sweet whistle and dog's quick yap
Woke the fox from out of his nap.

When I had written to this point in the tale I was most anxious to see a fox close at hand. I had not seen a fox for many years. There were many foxes in that countryside but they are usually night-moving animals and, being shyer than most wild things, they avoid mankind. Now I felt certain that morning that I should see a fox close-to if I walked Northward. So Northward I went into woodland. I found recent marks of foxes where they had furrowed-up the runs of mice. Beyond the wood, in moor and poor pasture, I found where they had eaten hedgehogs and left the prickly coats inside out. Though some of those relics were fresh and taint of fox was sometimes strong, I saw no fox alive. Turning West a little I looked along a great barren field with a pond at the end. At the pond's edge I saw a fox crouched. He was either drinking, as I supposed, or eating a water-fowl. There he is, I said to myself, but he will not let me come much nearer. I climbed over a fence and moved quietly towards him. He did not stir and I could not think why. I walked quickly towards him, but he did not move. Soon, when I could see that he had not been hunted, I knew that he must be dead. On coming to him at the water's edge I found that he was dead. But only just dead. His body was still warm and I judge that he may well have been alive when I'd set forth. He was the most beautiful dog-fox in faultless condition. It was from his body that I learned for the first time the beauty and the wonder of a fox's grace. I judged that he had picked up poison – plaster of Paris, perhaps – had come to drink at the pond and had died in drinking. From that moment I could write with greater certainty. I had, thenceforward, a deeper sympathy for a shy, wild, beautiful animal whose raids in springtime may be costly, whose voice in the midnight is satanic, but whose cleverness, even now, maintains him in a land that has nearly doubled her population in the last century. Let me now return to my fox as he roused, newly wakened by a lad with a terrier, in the Ghost Heath Stubs where he had slept.

He rose and stretched till the claws in his pads,
Stuck hornily out like long black gads,
He listened a while, and his nose went round
To catch the smell of the distant sound.

The windward smells came free from taint
They were rabbit, strongly, with lime-kiln, faint,
A wild-duck, likely, on Sars Holt Pond,
And sheep on the Sars Holt Down beyond.

The lee-ward smells were much less certain
For the Ghost Heath Hill was like a curtain,
Yet vague, from the lee-ward, now and then,
Came muffled sounds like the sound of men.

He moved to his right to a clearer space,
And all his soul came into his face,
Into his eyes and into his nose,
For over the hill a murmur rose.
His ears were cocked and his keen nose flaired,
He sneered with his lips till his teeth were bared,
He trotted right and lifted a pad
Trying to test what foes he had.

On Ghost Heath turf was a steady drumming
Which sounded like horses quickly coming,
It died as the hunt went down the dip,
Then Malapert yelped at Myngs' whip.
Then a burst of laughter, swiftly still,
Was muffled away by Ghost Heath Hill.
Then silence, then, in a burst, much clearer,
Voices and horses coming nearer,
And another noise, of a pit-pat-beat
On the Ghost Hill grass, of fox-hound feet.

He sat on his haunches listening hard,
While his mind went over the compass card,
Men were coming and rest was done,
But he still had time to get fit to run;
He could outlast horse and outrace hound,
But men were devils from Lobs' Pound.
And of all earth's ills, the ill least pleasant
Was to run in the light when men were present.
Men would follow from start to end,

Men were many, and none his friend,
Men who guess what a fox contrives:–
But still, needs must when the devil drives.

He readied himself, then a soft horn blew,
Then a clear voice carolled, 'Ed-Hoick. Eleu.'
Then the wood-end rang with the clear voice crying,
And the crackle of scrub where hounds were trying.
Then the horn blew nearer, a hound's voice quivered,
Then another, then more, and his body shivered.

He trotted down with his nose intent
For a fox's line to cross his scent,
It was only fair (he being a stranger)
That the native fox should have the danger.
Danger was coming, so swift, so swift,
That the pace of his trot began to lift.

He judged as he went the great wood through
He must break and run for the land he knew.

By the hounds in tongue; it was death to stay
He must make for home by the shortest way
But with all this yelling and all this wrath
And all these devils, how find a path?

He ran like a stag to the wood's north corner,
Where the hedge was thick and the ditch a yawner,
But the scarlet glimpse of Myngs on Turk,
Watching the woodside, made him shirk.

He ringed the wood and looked at the south.
What wind there was blew into his mouth.
But close to the woodland's blackthorn thicket
Was Dansey, still as a stone, on Picket.
And at Dansey's back were twenty more
Watching the cover and pressing fore.

The fox drew in and flaired with his muzzle.
Death was here if he messed the puzzle.
There were men without and hounds within,
A crying that stiffened the hair on skin,
Teeth in cover and death without,
Both deaths coming, and no way out.

His nose ranged swiftly, his heart beat fast,
Then a crashing cry rose up in a blast
Then the horn again made the hounds like mad
And a man, quite near, said, 'Found, by Gad,'
And a man, quite near, said, 'Now he'll break.
Lark's Leybourne Copse is the line he'll take.'
And men moved up with their talk and stink
And the traplike noise of the horseshoe clink.
Men whose coming meant death from teeth
In a worrying wrench with him beneath.

The fox sneaked down by the cover side,
(With his ears flexed back) as a snake would glide
He took the ditch at the cover-end,
He hugged the ditch as his only friend.
The blackbird cock with the golden beak
Got out of his way with a jabbering shriek
And the shriek told Tom on the raking bay
That for eighteen pence he was gone away.

He ran in the hedge in the triple growth
Of bramble and hawthorn, glad of both,
Till a couple of fields were past, and then
Came the living death of the dread of men.

Then, as he listened, he heard a 'Hoy,'
Tom Dansey's horn and 'Awa-wa-woy.'
Then all hounds crying with all their forces
Then a thundering down of seventy horses.
Robin Dawe's horn and halloos of 'Hey
Hark Hollar, Hoik' and 'Gone Away.'

Hounds were over and on his line
With a head like bees upon Tipple Tine.
The sound of the nearness sent a flood
Of terror of death through the fox's blood.
He upped his brush and he cocked his nose,
And he went upwind as a racer goes.

The fox was strong, he was full of running,
He could run for an hour and then use cunning,
But the cry behind him made him chill,
They would run him thus till they bit to kill.
Till he crouched back-up, dead-beat and dirty,

With nothing but teeth against the thirty.
And all the way to that blinding end
He would meet with men and have none his friend.
Men to holloa and men to run him,
With stones to stagger and yells to stun him,
Men to head him, with whips to beat him,
And hounds to mangle with mouths to eat him.
And all the way, with wild high crying,
To cold his blood with the thought of dying,
The horn and the cheer, and the drum-like thunder,
Of the horsehooves stamping the meadows under.
He upped his brush and went with a will
For the Sarsen Stones on Wan Dyke Hill.

Past Tineton Church over Tineton Waste,
With the lolloping ease of a fox's haste,
The fur on his chest blown dry with the air,
His brush still up and his cheek-teeth bare.
Over the Waste where the ganders grazed,
The long swift lilt of his loping lazed,
His ears cocked up as his blood ran higher,
He saw his point, and his eyes took fire.
The Wan Dyke Hill with its fir tree barren,
Its dark of gorse and its rabbit warren,
The Dyke on its heave like a tightened girth,
And holes in the Dyke where a fox might earth.
He had rabbited there long months before,
The earths were deep and his need was sore,
The way was new, but he took a bearing,
And rushed like a blown ship billow-sharing.

Off Tineton Common to Tineton Dean,
Where the wind-hid elders pushed with green;
Through the Dean's thin cover across the lane,
And up Midwinter to King of Spain.
Old Joe at digging his garden grounds,
Said, 'A fox, being hunted; where be hounds?
O lord, my back, to be young again,
'Stead a zellin zider in King of Spain.
O hark, I hear 'em, O sweet, O sweet.
Why there be redcoat on Gearge's wheat.
And there be redcoat, and there they gallop.
Thur go a browncoat down a wallop.
Quick, Ellen, Quick, Come Susan, fly.

Here'm hounds. I zeed the fox go by,
Go by like thunder, go by like blasting,
With his girt white teeth all looking ghasting.
There's huntsman, there. The fox come past,
(As I was a-digging) as fast as fast.
He's only been gone a minute by;
A girt dark dog as pert as pye.'

Ellen and Susan came out scattering
Brooms and dustpans till all was clattering;
They saw the pack come head to foot
Running like racers, nearly mute;
Robin and Dansey quartering near,
All going gallop like startled deer.
Red coats and dark coats thrusting and spurring,
Sending the partridge coveys whirring,
Then a rattle up hill and a clop up lane,
It emptied the bar of the King of Spain.

Tom left his cider, Dick left his bitter,
Granfer James left his pipe and spitter,
Out they came from the sawdust floor,
They said, 'They'm going.' They said, 'O Lor.'

The fox raced on, across Barton Balks,
With a crackle of kex in the nettle stalks,
By Polly's folly, and Gaunts, and Sheres,
And the Oasts like women, with hooded ears,
Past Abbots Ashes, and Beggars Oak,
Through cutters' and layers' bonfire-smoke,
Past Maddings Hollow, down Dundry Dip,
And up Goose Grass to the Sailing Ship.

The three black firs of the Ship stood still
On the bare chalk heave of the Dundry Hill,
The fox looked back as he slackened past
The scaled red-bole of the mizen-mast.

There they were coming, mute but swift,
A scarlet smear in the blackthorn rift,
A white horse rising, a dark horse flying,
And the hungry hounds too tense for crying.
Stormcock leading, his stern spear-straight,
Racing as though for a piece of plate,

Little speck horsemen field on field;
Then Dansey viewed him and Robin squealed.

At the 'View Halloo' the hounds went frantic,
Back went Stormcock and up went Antic,
Up went Skylark as Antic sped
It was zest to blood how they carried head.
Skylark drooped as Maroon drew by,
But their hackles lifted, they scored to cry.

The fox knew well, that before they tore him,
They should try their speed on the downs before him,
There were three more miles to the Wan Dyke Hill,
And his heart was high, that he beat them still.
The wind of the downland charmed his bones
So off he went for the Sarsen Stones.

The pure clean air came sweet to his lungs,
He thought foul scorn of those crying tongues,
In three miles more he would reach the haven
In the Wan Dyke croaked on by the raven,
In three miles more he would make his berth
On the hard cool floor of a Wan Dyke earth,
Too deep for spade, too curved for terrier,
With the pride of the race to make rest the merrier.
In three miles more he would reach his dream,
So his game heart gulped and he put on steam.

Like a rocket shot to a ship ashore,
The lean red bolt of his body tore,
Like a ripple of wind running swift on grass,
Like a shadow on wheat when a cloud blows past,
Like a turn at the buoy in a cutter sailing,
When the bright green gleam lips white at the railing,
Like the April snake whipping back to sheath,
Like the gannets' hurtle on fish beneath,
Like a kestrel chasing, like a sickle reaping,
Like all things swooping, like all things sweeping,
Like a hound for stay, like a stag for swift,
With his shadow beside like spinning drift.

Past the gibbet-stock all stuck with nails,
Where they hanged in chains what had hung at jails,
Past Ashmundshowe where Ashmund sleeps,

And none but the tumbling peewit weeps,
Past Curlew Calling, the gaunt grey corner
Where the curlew comes as a summer mourner,
Past Blowbury Beacon shaking his fleece,
Where all winds hurry and none brings peace,
Then down, on the mile-long green decline
Where the turf's like spring and the air's like wine,
Where the sweeping spurs of the downland spill
Into Wan Brook Valley and Wan Dyke Hill.

The blood in his veins went romping high
'Get on, on, on to the earth or die.'
The air of the downs went purely past,
And he felt the glory of going fast,
Till the terror of death, though there indeed,
Was lulled for a while by his pride of speed,
He was romping away from hounds and hunt,
He had Wan Dyke Hill and his earth in front,
In one mile more when his point was made,
He would rest in safety from dog or spade,
Nose between paws he would hear the shout
Of the 'Gone to earth' to the hounds without,
The whine of the hounds, and their cat-feet gadding,
Scratching the earth, and their breath pad-padding,
He would hear the horn call hounds away,
And rest in peace till another day.

In one mile more he would lie at rest,
So for one mile more he would go his best.
He reached the dip at the long droop's end
And he took what speed he had still to spend.

As he raced the corn towards Wan Dyke Brook,
The pack had view of the way he took,
Robin hallooed from the downland's crest,
He capped them on till they did their best.
That quarter-mile to the Wan Brook's brink
Was raced as quick as a man can think.

And here, as he ran to the huntsman's yelling,
The fox first felt that the pace was telling,
His body and lungs seemed all grown old,
His legs less certain, his heart less bold,
The hound-noise nearer, the hill slope steeper,

The thud in the blood of his body deeper,
His pride in his speed, his joy in the race
Were withered away, for what use was pace?
He had run his best, and the hounds ran better.
Then the going worsened, the ground was wetter.
Then his brush drooped down till it sometimes dragged
And his fur felt sick and his chest was tagged
With taggles of mud, and his pads seemed lead,
It was well for him he'd an earth ahead.

Down he went to the brook and over,
Out of the corn and into the clover,
Over the slope that the Wan Brook drains,
Past Battle Tump where they earthed the Danes,
Then up the hill that the Wan Dyke rings
Where the Sarsen Stones stand grand like kings.

There were seven Sarsens of granite grim,
As he ran them by they looked at him;
As he leaped the lip of their earthen paling
The hounds were gaining and he was failing.

He was still ahead by a furlong clear.
But oh the joy that his earth was near.
From the rampart's edge he scampered down
To the deep green ditch of the dead men's town.

Within, as he reached that soft green turf,
The wind, blowing lonely, moaned like surf,
Desolate ramparts rose up steep,
On either side, for the ghosts to keep.
He passed the spring where the rushes spread,
And there in the stones was his earth ahead.
One last short burst upon failing feet,
There life lay waiting, so sweet, so sweet,
Rest in a darkness, balm for aches.

The earth was stopped. It was barred with stakes.

Though every fox in a hunting country knows that likely earths are
stopped, the shock of finding one stopped when hounds are near
must be shattering. It was so to this fox. But he knew that within a
hundred yards of him, in the same trench, was another burrow. He

had no time to think it over – no choice – he had to run for it at once. On he went just round the bend in the trench to an even worse shock. He ran straight into a party of young men with guns and dogs who were putting a ferret down the very burrow he hoped to enter. A lad loosed a terrier at the fox. The terrier flew at him and the fox raced away downhill into a spinney. No terrier, of course, could outrace a fox. And as the lads recalled their dog and the fox lay panting, the hounds and hunt came up on the hill above and checked. The fox, on the instant, knew that he was not being hunted. Hounds were puzzled. Scent is a mysterious property, subject to certain interferences such as altered soil, shift of wind or change of temperature. It is sensitively subject to interruptions of its line by other scent: petrol, red herring, aniseed. The hounds, in this instance, were utterly puzzled by the scent of the terrier. They could make nothing of it. The huntsman tried a cast which failed. The fox had, therefore, some minutes of peace. After recovering from his fright and drawing breath he moved leisurely away towards another safe shelter in a distant wood. After the cast failed the huntsmen lifted hounds away to a likely line on which they gave tongue. The fox knew, at once, that they were after him again. He was well-breathed but he had spent most of his strength. He was still nearly four miles from his shelter in the rocks and could not hope to out-run hounds in a race so long. He had to try to outwit them by cunning. He began to 'run short', as it is called, using one clever trick after another. First he ran among sheep hoping that the smell of the sheep would confuse the hounds. The huntsmen viewed him through the sheep and held the hounds after him. Next he ran into a brook hoping that the water might kill his scent. Two little boys saw him and called the huntsmen. He was still about two miles from his shelter in the Mourne End Woods. The land before him was in big, open, tree-less fields, rising gradually to a hill-top with the wood a little to the Westward from the crest. There, in the wood, was his shelter if he could reach it. He left the reeds of the Morton Pond and ran towards it.

The ducks flew up from the Morton Pond.
The fox looked up at their tailing strings,
He wished (perhaps) that a fox had wings.
Wings with his friends in a great V straining
The autumn sky when the moon is gaining;
For better the grey sky's solitude,
Than to be two miles from the Mourne End Wood
With the hounds behind, clean-trained to run,

And your strength half spent and your breath half gone.
Better the reeds and the sky and water
Than that hopeless pad from a certain slaughter,
At the Morton Pond the fields began,
Long Tew's green meadows; he ran; he ran.

First the six green fields that make a mile,
With the lip-full Clench at the side the while,
With rooks above, slow-circling, shewing
The world of men where a fox was going;
To all things else he was dumb and blind,
Save the grass ahead and the hounds behind.

At the last green field was the long slow climb,
To the Mourne End Wood, as old as time;
Yew woods dark, where they cut for bows,
Oak woods green with the mistletoes,
Dark woods evil, but burrowed deep
With a brock's earth strong, where a fox might sleep.
He felt the heave of the hill grow stiff,
He saw black woods, which would shelter – if –
The line of hope upon Mourne Hill brow,
A mile, three-quarters, a half-mile now.

Four hundred yards, and the worst was past,
The slope was gentler and shorter-grassed.
Two hundred yards, and the running thence
Was an almost flat to the Mourne End fence.
One hundred yards, but the hounds had viewed
They gasped to kill him outside the wood.

The trees drew over him dark like Norns,
He was over the ditch and at the thorns.

He thrust the thorns, but they would not yield,
He leaped, and fell, in sight of the field,
A gurgle of joy showed hounds aware
That they saw their quarry before them there.

He gathered himself for a new attempt,
His life before was an old dream dreamt,
His life to come was a gleam of wit
To reach the burrow before they bit.

In his extremity of terror and exhaustion his cunning mind knew one device more: to get over the fence and swerve instantly sharply to one side and then race for his burrow in the hope that the hounds, in their rush, might miss the swerve and run on a hundred yards or more before they found their error. It was his one chance with one instant left in which to snatch it.

He gathered himself, he leaped, he reached
The top of the hedge like a fish-boat beached.
He balanced a second and then leaped down
To the dark of the yews where daylights drown.

His luck for the minute held: the hounds did over-run his line and the huntsmen failed to be with them for that minute.

For a minute he ran and heard no sound,
Then a whimper came from a questing hound,
Then a huntsman halloed, and then 'Leu Leu,'
The floating laugh of the horn that blew.
Then the very air of the woods seemed cry,
And his earth so far that he needs must die,
Die where he reeled in the woodland dim
With a hound's white grips in the spine of him.
For one more burst he could spurt, and then
Wait for the teeth, and the wrench, and men.

He made his spurt for the Mourne End rocks,
The air blew rank with the taint of fox;
The yews gave way to a greener space
Of great stones strewn in a grassy place.
And there was his earth at the great grey shoulder,
Sunk in the ground, of a granite boulder.
A dry deep burrow with rocky roof,
Proof against crowbars, terrier-proof,
Life to the dying, rest for bones.

The earth was stopped; it was filled with stones.

Then, for a moment, his courage failed,
His eyes looked up as his body quailed,
Then the coming of death, which all things dread,
Made him run for the wood ahead.

The taint of fox was rank on the air,
He knew, as he ran, there were foxes there.
His strength was broken, his heart was bursting,
His bones were rotten, his throat was thirsting,
His feet were reeling, his brush was thick
From dragging the mud, and his brain was sick.

He thought as he ran of his old delight
In the wood in the moon in an April night,
His happy hunting, his winter loving,
The smells of things in the midnight roving,
The look of his dainty-nosing, red
Clean-felled dam with her footpad's tread,
Of his sire, so swift, so game, so cunning,
With craft in his brain and power of running,
Their fights of old when his teeth drew blood.
Now he was sick, with his coat all mud.

He crossed the covert, he crawled the bank,
To a meuse in the thorns and there he sank,
With his ears flexed back and his teeth shown white,
In a rat's resolve for a dying bite.

And there, as he lay, he saw the vale,
That a struggling sunlight silvered pale,
The Deerlip Brook like a strip of steel,
The Nun's Wood Yews where the rabbits squeal,
The great grass square of the Roman Fort,
And the smoke in the elms at Crendon Court.

And above the smoke in the elm-tree tops,
Was the beech-clump's blur, Blown Hilcote Copse,
Where he and his mates had long made merry
In the bloody joys of the rabbit-herry.

And there as he lay and looked, the cry
Of the hounds at head came rousing by;
He bent his bones in the blackthorn dim –

But the cry of the hounds was not for him.
Over the fence with a crash they went,
Belly to grass, with a burning scent,
Then came Dansey, yelling to Bob,
'They've changed at Ruckit, now here's a job.'

104

And Bob yelled back, 'Well, we cannot turn 'em,
It's Jumper and Antic, Tom; we'll learn 'em.
We must just go on, and I hope we kill.'
They followed hounds down the Mourne End Hill.

The fox lay still in the rabbit-meuse,
On the dry brown dust of the plumes of yews.
In the bottom below a brook went by,
Blue, in a patch, like a streak of sky.
There, one by one, with a clink of stone
Came a red or dark coat on a horse half blown.
And man to man with a gasp for breath
Said, 'Lord, what a run. I'm fagged to death.'

After an hour, no riders came,
The day drew by like an ending game;
A robin sang from a pufft red breast,
The fox lay quiet and took his rest.
A wren on a tree-stump carolled clear,
Then the starlings wheeled in a sudden sheer,
The rooks came home to the twiggy hive
In the elm-tree tops which the winds do drive.
Then the noise of the rooks fell slowly still,
And the lights came out in the Clench Brook Mill;
Then a pheasant cocked, then an owl began
With the cry that curdles the blood of man.

The stars grew bright as the yews grew black,
The fox rose stiffly and stretched his back.
He flaired the air, then he padded out
To the valley below him dark as doubt,
Winter-thin with the young green crops,
For Old Cold Crendon and Hilcote Copse.

As he crossed the meadows at Naunton Larking,
The dogs in the town all started barking,
For with feet all bloody and flanks all foam,
The hounds and the hunt were limping home;
Limping home in the dark, dead-beaten,
The hounds all rank from a fox they'd eaten,
Dansey saying to Robin Dawe,
'The fastest and longest I ever saw.'
And Robin answered, 'O Tom, 't was good,
I thought they'd changed in the Mourne End Wood,

But now I feel that they did not change.
We've had a run that was great and strange;
And to kill in the end, at dusk, on grass.
We'll turn to The Cock and take a glass,
For the hounds, poor souls, are past their forces.
And a gallon of ale for our poor horses,
And some bits of bread for the hounds, poor things,
After all they've done (for they've done like kings),
Would keep them going till we get in.
We had it alone from Nun's Wood Whin.'
Then Tom replied, 'If they changed or not,
There've been few runs longer and none more hot,
We shall talk of today until we die.'

The stars grew bright in the winter sky,
The wind came keen with a tang of frost,
The brook was troubled for new things lost,
The copse was happy for old things found,
The fox came home and he went to ground.

And the hunt came home and the hounds were fed,
They climbed to their bench and went to bed,
The horses in stable loved their straw.
'Good-night, my beauties,' said Robin Dawe.

Then the moon came quiet and flooded full
Light and beauty on clouds like wool,
On a feasted fox at rest from hunting,
In the beech wood grey where the brocks were grunting.

The beech wood grey rose dim in the night
With moonlight fallen in pools of light,
The long-dead leaves on the ground were rimed.
A clock struck twelve and the church-bells chimed.

Source: *A Fox's Day*, London: Argo Record Company Limited (RG224), transcribed by PWE.

LP Record Sleeve Note from A Fox's Day, 1960

The story, *Reynard the Fox*, some of which makes the foundation of this record, was written in Berkshire and published in London in the year 1919.

I had been thinking, for some time, of a peaceful theme that would show English society as a unity seemingly as complete as the unity of Chaucer's pilgrims.

Perhaps the unity of those pilgrims was not very close at any time of the pilgrimage; but one purpose had brought them together, so that Chaucer could survey all the main branches of English life, and make each clear to us in the great Prologue of his design.

In 1919, no pilgrimage attracted our society, nor had we much incentive to unity: indeed, there seemed a plentiful incentive everywhere to rebellion, anarchy and disruption.

At the time, it seemed to me that only in the fox-hunt would the main branches of our society meet and mix actively together with good will and fellow feeling in a peaceful enterprise that might make a story.

At the time, I knew nothing of fox-hunting, but I had often seen it in childhood, had followed it, on foot, sometimes, in early boyhood, and had a lively memory of its beauty as a winter pageant in woods and fields.

To improve this frail foundation I read what books I could find upon the subject (there are plenty of these) and questioned what hunting men I knew.

To all of these last my indebtedness is very great, for all of them, though not one of them suspected it, was a moving poet when talking of his delight. I found a lesser ecstasy in some of the better books on the theme.

After forty years, it is clear that English country life has greatly changed. The last meet that I saw was much unlike the one that I describe. The population has increased; new amusements have come; easy travel has spread suburbs over many miles of country; and, with all this the costs of hunting have grown past telling.

Though change is everywhere, the main character of my tale, the Fox, survives.

His shy, sly, clever, beautiful and murderous grace still moves in the country-side startling the night with the ghastly shriek of his joy, and, in Springtime, feathering the fields in the ecstasies of a successful pounce.

Source: *A Fox's Day*, London: Argo Record Company Limited, 1960 (RG 224).

Introduction, 1962

The story *Reynard the Fox* was written in the year 1919 at Boars Hill, in Berkshire.

As a child, living within half a mile of a kennel of fox-hounds, I had often seen both hounds and huntsmen. As a boy I had sometimes followed hounds on foot from a meet to a covert, had seen the fox away, and (now and then) had judged the chances and seen rather more. But when wishing to write of a fox-hunt, this scanty and remote knowledge did not serve. I knew that I knew nothing about it, and set myself to learn from the many books that exist upon the matter, and from a few friends to whom hunting was the breath of life.

It had been a part of my design to show the characters composing an English country society (such as had existed before the War) all together at once. As far as my knowledge went, this much mixed society could be seen all together only at a fox-hunt. At the time of my writing, this country society had already much changed from what I had seen and known as a child.

My knowledge of foxes was of the slightest, for foxes are shy, night-moving animals. I had seen (I believe) only two or three un-hunted foxes in all my life. Soon after I had begun to write the story, I was made to feel, in a strange and happy way, that something not before known to me, some Sympathy, something (shall we say?) akin to the Tutelary Spirit of Foxes, was there to help. Soon, when I wished to see a Fox close-to, I found a beautiful dog-fox, still warm, dead (I feel sure from poison) at a Berkshire pond-side. A week or two later, a vixen laid-up her cubs in my garden; and a little later, a poor fox caught in a gin-trap knew me for a friend and let me release him, without giving me the expected bite.

But though a hunted fox was my subject, it was but the image of my subject. For more than four years before I wrote, something primitive, wild, beautiful and strange in the Spirit of Man had been pursued through most of Europe with the threat of death. It had survived the chase, but as a hunted fox may survive a long run, to lie panting somewhere till the heart stops beating. It was my hope that my Fox's heart should not stop beating.

Source: 'Introduction', *Dauber & Reynard the Fox*, London: William Heine-mann, 1962, pp. 77–78.

The Hunt, 1966

A short half mile from my home on the east side of the road to Bosbury, and well back from that road, so that they could not be seen from the road, were the kennels of the Ledbury Hounds. The hounds and stables of some of the staff of the Hunt lay near the kennels, a little further north.

I saw the hounds at exercise very frequently and would sometimes see them, or some of their followers, in or near the coverts on that side of their country. They figured largely in my interests and admirations, but not so largely as the canal and the life of the canal.

In the hunting season I often saw them setting forth to or coming back from a hunt. Sometimes a rider would be with them coming home, with a fox's mask as his trophy strapped to his saddle. Once when I was very young, I was amazed and delighted to find the hunt, hounds, huntsmen and riders all thrusting into our field and checked at the garden fence, and seeking leave to come through after their fox.

This was an unexpected wonder, but there the hounds and hunt servants were, at check at the fence, with fifty or sixty riders streaming up the field to them. The hounds had been called off just in time, or they would have been all over the garden and out on the other side. There they were, not too well-pleased at being stopped, and there were the Huntsman and the Master asking leave to come through to the road; and the crowd of riders increasing under my eyes.

They had come on a hot scent down the westerly wind, and there they all were; the hounds vexed, and perhaps earning a rate or two, and some little delay in the coming of the permission to come through: a minute perhaps (which I enjoyed if the hounds didn't). Then, at a word the gates opened, and the Huntsman gave the word, trailing his whiplash and with the word from him the hounds were at his horse's heels, and every possible care was given to the garden by those who took its two ways to the road. Hounds and followers were on the road in a couple of minutes, but they could not make anything of their fox there. Something had killed the scent in the few minutes of the check, perhaps cattle on the road, or other traffic. They had to lift hounds and try some of the great coverts of the Frith.

The wonder of the sight, the eager hounds fresh and excited by the half mile of their hunt (for they had found at Wall Hills), and the joy of seeing all the hunt so near at hand, and so near a fox who yet was then out of danger, stirred me to paint a picture of the scene, over which I took great pains, and much red paint.

Early in every year the kennels made use of a field near the railway station as the birthplace and breeding-quarters of the pack. The place was given over to little kennels, each with privacy and a special run, and conspicuous notices to the public:

'Beware of the Hound Bitches
Very Dangerous.'

Source: 'The Hunt', *Grace Before Ploughing*, London: William Heinemann, 1966, pp. 39–40.

Fyfield*Books*

Two millennia of essential classics
The extensive Fyfield*Books* list includes

Djuna Barnes *The Book of Repulsive Women and other poems*
edited by Rebecca Loncraine

Elizabeth Barrett Browning *Selected Poems* edited by Malcolm Hicks

Charles Baudelaire *Complete Poems in French and English*
translated by Walter Martin

Thomas Lovell Beddoes *Death's Jest-Book* edited by Michael Bradshaw

Aphra Behn *Selected Poems*
edited by Malcolm Hicks

Border Ballads: A Selection
edited by James Reed

The Brontë Sisters *Selected Poems*
edited by Stevie Davies

Sir Thomas Browne *Selected Writings*
edited by Claire Preston

Lewis Carroll *Selected Poems*
edited by Keith Silver

Paul Celan *Collected Prose*
translated by Rosmarie Waldrop

Thomas Chatterton *Selected Poems*
edited by Grevel Lindop

John Clare *By Himself*
edited by Eric Robinson and David Powell

Arthur Hugh Clough *Selected Poems*
edited by Shirley Chew

Samuel Taylor Coleridge *Selected Poetry* edited by William Empson and David Pirie

Tristan Corbière *The Centenary Corbière*
in French and English
translated by Val Warner

William Cowper *Selected Poems*
edited by Nick Rhodes

Gabriele d'Annunzio *Halcyon*
translated by J.G. Nichols

John Donne *Selected Letters*
edited by P.M. Oliver

William Dunbar *Selected Poems*
edited by Harriet Harvey Wood

Anne Finch, Countess of Winchilsea *Selected Poems*
edited by Denys Thompson

Ford Madox Ford *Selected Poems*
edited by Max Saunders

John Gay *Selected Poems*
edited by Marcus Walsh

Oliver Goldsmith *Selected Writings*
edited by John Lucas

Robert Herrick *Selected Poems*
edited by David Jesson-Dibley

Victor Hugo *Selected Poetry*
in French and English
translated by Steven Monte

T.E. Hulme *Selected Writings*
edited by Patrick McGuinness

Leigh Hunt *Selected Writings*
edited by David Jesson Dibley

Wyndham Lewis *Collected Poems and Plays* edited by Alan Munton

Charles Lamb *Selected Writings*
edited by J.E. Morpurgo

Lucretius *De Rerum Natura: The Poem on Nature*
translated by C.H. Sisson

For more information, including a full list of Fyfield*Books* and a contents list for each title, and details of how to order the books, visit the Carcanet website at www.carcanet.co.uk or email info@carcanet.co.uk